Eight at the Top

Eight at the Top

A View Inside Public Education

Gloria L. Johnston
Gwen E. Gross
Rene S. Townsend
Peggy Lynch
Patricia B. Novotney
Benita Roberts
Lorraine Garcy
Libia Gil

A ScarecrowEducation Book
Published in partnership with the
American Association of School Administrators

The Scarecrow Press, Inc.
Lanham, Maryland, and London
2002

A SCARECROWEDUCATION BOOK
Published in partnership with
the American Association of School Administrators

Published in the United States of America
by Scarecrow Press, Inc.
A Member of the Rowman & Littlefield Publishing Group
4720 Boston Way, Lanham, Maryland 20706
www.scarecroweducation.com

4 Pleydell Gardens, Folkestone
Kent CT20 2DN, England

British Library Cataloguing in Publication Information Available

Library of Congress Cataloging-in-Publication Data

Eight at the top : a view inside public education / Gloria L. Johnston ... [et.al.].
    p.   cm.
    Includes index.
    ISBN 0-8108-4215-7 (pbk. : alk. paper)
    1.   School superintendents-United States-Anecdotes. 2. Educational
leadership-United States-Anecdotes. I. Johnston, Gloria L., 1947-

LB2831.72 .E54 2002
371.2'011-dc21
                                                                2001049654

⊖™ The paper used in this publication meets the minimum requirements of
American National Standard for Information Sciences—Permanence of
Paper for Printed Library Materials, ANSI/NISO Z39.48-1992.
Manufactured in the United States of America.

Contents

v

Foreword

STORY (stôrë) n., pl. -ries.
1. An account of incidents or events 2. A fictional narrative shorter than a novel 3. A widely circulated rumor 4. A lie, falsehood 5. Legend, romance 6. A news article of broadcast 7. Matter, situation

Webster's Collegiate Dictionary

Good leaders must understand and use the power of stories. That is because stories have the power to transport the reader to another time and place, to place the reader in the life of the storyteller, and to bring theory to life. Stories help us organize our thoughts, bring pattern and order to random happenings, and frame our world. Stories can be the common thread that joins disparate and diverse people together. Stories have the capacity to connect the head with the heart.

Eight superintendents came together over a period of months to share their stories with each other, and now, with their readers. They examine their experiences as superintendents through five distinct lenses, each one an important organizing framework for leadership.

They talk about knowing the community, the board, the organization and its people, the students, and finally yourself. Each section includes stories of individual people and their unique community and concludes with "Lessons Learned."

These superintendents—all women—write with candor and wisdom about their successes and their mistakes. They talk about why they chose

to leave their positions as principals, where all were happy and successful, to take on the challenges of the superintendency. They write with
honesty about what it takes to survive and thrive as a superintendent.
The dominant theme throughout their writing is how critical the importance of listening long and hard before acting is. They say that the "community owns the schools" and that a superintendent must hear the community and its goals for its children.

They do not flinch from the formidable task of working with their
boards, stressing that there are no shortcuts to developing relationships
of trust with each board member.

Good storytellers are good listeners. They hear the meanings and nu-
ances behind the spoken word and help the reader hear them, too. *Eight
at the Top* will remind school system leaders why they chose this profession and inspire others to take on the important work of leaderships.

Paul D. Houston
Executive Director, American Association of School Administrators

Quotes from the Authors

Rene Townsend: "The invitation to work with a group of women leaders was intriguing; and reflecting and writing are two of my favorite activities. As a lifelong student of leadership and a passionate supporter of education, teaching, and learning, there wasn't another possible answer than an unequivocal 'yes' to the invitation."

Benita Roberts: "The first three years of my superintendency were indeed painful. This was not something I expected to encounter. The majority of my board members had known me for years, and as a result, I thought that they and members of my community understood my values and would recognize that I would always behave in a principled manner. However, when a few personnel and community issues emerged, they appeared to forget our past relationship and blamed me. Later, I discovered this was a common reaction, but I felt that other superintendents or aspiring superintendents might gain from my experiences; therefore, I became part of the writing group."

Peggy Lynch: "First, I was intrigued with the concept of documenting our superintendent experiences in a publication. Even though I was skeptical about generating interest in other readers, the thought of meeting with highly successful women leaders in education and the opportunity to learn from their accomplishments were extremely appealing. The time of this project came during my observation that many superintendents appeared to be more focused on self-promotion

rather than self-improvement. I was anxious to establish collegial relationships with individuals who have a passionate sense of purpose and
shared values for educating our children."

Gwen Gross: "For several years I'd harbored a private fantasy of becoming an author. I've always thought that writing books for children
would be a particularly rewarding experience. Toward that goal, I enrolled in a series of wonderful classes taught by a well-regarded author.
I loved the classes. We read hundreds of books, studied successful authors, and discovered what sparked imagination. Our instructor told us
that we should write from our innermost memories. I have been touched
many times by the learning that occurs when reaching out to others and
decided I wanted to share what I feel and the techniques that I rely on
when faced with tough challenges. I hoped that some of the lessons I
have learned will provide guidance to colleagues who have been as fortunate as I to have chosen education as a profession."

Lorraine Garcy: "In our daily role we are consumed with action-
oriented activities which leaves little or no time for reflection. It was exciting to consider a project that would generate time for self-reflection
as well as the power of sharing individual and collective thoughts. I
was uncertain about the process to reach our goal, but this unknown
contributed to the excitement and adventure for personal challenge,
development, and growth."

Patricia Novotney: "My initial reaction to participation in a book
was 'yes, sure!' Upon further thought, the following issues and questions came to mind:

- Who else would participate?
- How long would the participation take?
- What would the structure/format of the book be?
- Would everybody have to agree in philosophy?
- Would this book be one of theory, practice, or a combination?
- Would work be distributed equally?

As is evident, the questions were more technical in nature; however,
the overwhelming gut response was that I have some very personal beliefs and have had a wide variety of experiences that might benefit an

aspiring and/or current administrator. Let's tell the story and let's have it be a real one."

Libia Gil: "I was very excited with the prospect of writing a book about superintendent conversations. I had always wanted to have something I had written published, but never expected to have the chance. I was also intrigued with the idea of working with other superintendents on this project. Many questions went through my mind: Would I write well enough for this project? Would I be able to make the commitment necessary? How would eight diverse people work together to finish the project? I said yes, even with all my unanswered questions."

Gloria Johnston: "When I finally finished my dissertation about the work of public school superintendents, I knew I wanted to write for a larger audience. It took me several years to finally make a proposal to a group of colleagues. I was surprised that each woman I asked to participate in a 'book writing project' agreed. What started out as an academic extension of my research turned out to be one of the most enriching professional and personal development experiences of my life."

Preface

"Very little is known about the superintendent's present condition, or what past and present superintendents believe." (Carter and Cunningham, 1997)

"Despite the common perception that superintendents are key figures in school systems, they remain largely shrouded in mystery." (Wirt, 1991)

"The superintedency is more than knowing how to do, it is knowing how to think and how to feel." (Kennert and Augenstein, 1990)

More than 15,000 superintendents lead school districts across the United States, yet information about the day-to-day work of these professionals is still relatively scarce. Books and studies about superintendents and the superintendency have been written mainly by doctoral candidates and university researchers/professors with limited or no experience as school superintendents.

We wanted to talk about the work of superintendents from the inside, as it is experienced by practicing superintendents. Using a folkloric, storytelling model, we wrote "on the job" stories—situations we lived and the lessons we learned from reflecting on these experiences. Before we wrote, we talked, sharing our life stories— who we were, what we cared about, and how we ended up as eight of the 15,000.

Our stories are about a job none of us started out to hold. Not surprisingly, we began our careers as teachers for the universal reason people become teachers, to work with children and make a difference. Later, we moved into administration to make a greater contribution.

Our trajectories differed. Some of us followed a traditional route from assistant principal to principal, then to the central office as directors or assistant superintendents, and finally to superintendents. One went directly from principal to superintendent.

To a person, we loved being principals. So why did we keep going to become superintendents? There is, of course, no one answer, but two dominant reasons were the desire to have a larger sphere of influence and a belief that somehow we could do the job not just as well, but better than we saw it being done.

The irony is, we all gave up some of the things we liked best—the fun and important work of touching young lives directly, day in and day out, as teachers and principals. But one school is a microcosm of the bigger educational picture, and eventually we yearned to be in that bigger scene.

We were impelled forward by positive and negative forces. Mentors influenced us in life-changing ways. Some of us were told by our superintendents, "You need to become a superintendent, and you need to start getting ready now." We watched these mentors and other top superintendents to get an idea of what was in store for us, and we were grateful for their strong modeling. They gave us an indelible image of what the position should be like and the motivation to try for it.

For some, a powerful impetus came from educational or training programs—an innovative university doctoral program, a district-wide leadership training retreat, a state superintendency academy, a national "Superintendents Prepared" program, even a Dale Carnegie course on "How to Win Friends and Influence People."

Our experiences underscored what it took to be successful educational leaders, and helped us realize we had the strengths, skills, knowledge—and desire—to take on this demanding role. Most importantly, we believed we could accomplish vital goals as we continued to develop the critical art and skills of leadership for this people-intensive work. We are good at communicating because we have to, and we like to. We're good at motivation, persuasion, building relationships, uniting people, and creating a team. People respond positively to our inclusive styles.

Educational practitioners are doers. We crave action and we know how to organize. But we are also big-picture people who think, analyze and reflect in a continuous, interweaving fashion.

Some of our greatest strengths are our abilities to listen, tolerate ambiguity, handle conflict, and confront new challenges. Other strengths are more intangible, and have to do with core values and belief systems, with ethics and moral leadership, and with a willingness and absolute commitment to take responsibility for the next generation. We are passionate about what we do, and we love our work as advocates for children and youth.

What started as a sourcebook directed at "What I wished I knew before I became a superintendent . . ." ended up as a set of stories moving from the bigger scene inward to reflect on ourselves. We are committed to on-going learning via reading, formal conferences, seminars, and dialogues with colleagues. This book is an outgrowth of our dedication to professional growth.

The content represents a universality of experience—broken into discrete chapters. We start with the larger perspective of Knowing Your Community, move systematically inward to Knowing Your Board, and continue on to Knowing Your Organization and Its People and Knowing Your Students. The final chapter leads the reader closest to the core of the superintendency—Knowing Yourself.

Knowing Your Community leads with advice about getting to know the larger community of the school district when you are new to the position. The stories highlight the diversity of communities, moves on to the importance of developing relationships, and ends with experiences related to the impact of the media.

Knowing Your Board starts with a critical message for superintendents—know your bosses! Stories focus on the importance of building the board as a team and the age-old debate about the line between policy and administration. The chapter ends with a discussion of public board meetings.

Knowing Your Organization and Its People highlights critical leadership skills in stories that relate to the actions and decisions you make from your very first day as a superintendent. We stress the requisite day-to-day knowledge and skills, and also emphasize the importance of looking to the future.

Knowing Your Students goes to the heart, the true focus of our work. We write about how and what we do for students, and what they do for us. As we told our stories to each other, this chapter more than any other, brought shared tears, laughter and passionate agreement about our work on behalf of children.

Finally, the chapter Knowing Yourself reaches the soul of superintendency. We tell you a lot about ourselves as we describe some painful and significant experiences. We reveal our personal qualities, describe how we survive some of the toughest times, and express our core values and beliefs.

At the end of each chapter, we attempt to tell you what we learned as superintendents by living these experiences, and by sharing these stories with one another. We hope these lessons will be valuable to you no matter what your position or role with children or schools. We hope you'll draw out additional lessons that have meaning for your thinking, your current role, and your role in the future. Most of all, we hope our work will cause you to think about your own amazing stories and reinvigorate your commitment to serving children. Make no mistake about it, the work of educators is the most important work to be done in a democracy.

Note: Names and schools have been changed throughout to protect privacy. The authors wish to thank Karen Ise for her work in typing and organizing the material.

Chapter 1

Knowing Your Community

"Researching a potential new community and school district can be a wonderful adventure."

The power of a supportive community and a superintendent's success cannot be underestimated.

When successful superintendents are asked what they feel has been an essential component to their support within the community, they always respond that they took time to embrace every community organization that interacts with the school system. From service clubs, to places of worship, to other educational institutions, to the media, superintendents knew forming alliances was the key. In good times these community groups reach out and support opportunities for students, and in difficult times they continue to form a wide network of support on which to rely. When a superintendent has connections with both breadth and depth among community organizations, a wide range of people feel connected to the district and its leader.

In learning about a new community, you must do your homework. Every community has a unique culture full of history and pride. The wise superintendent knows this. An even wiser new superintendent takes the time to carefully observe, listen, document and reflect on existing structures. Most importantly, the wise superintendent embraces this community spirit and pride by affirming the history of the community.

DO YOUR RESEARCH

Learning about a New Community

Researching a potential new community and school district can be a wonderful adventure. There is nothing quite as exciting as finding out if the new opportunity you are considering is a match with your background of training, experiences and personal talents. Learning about the community is an on-going process. Forgetting to continually update your information about the community can lead to unforeseen, and sometimes negative, consequences. Let me weave a story of how I approached a new position.

The position announcement was printed in the statewide listing of job opportunities. I called the search firm and obtained the brochure which described the geographical setting of the community and the demographic data of the school district. The brochure included the mission and goals for the district followed by descriptions of professional and personal qualities desired in the new superintendent.

At the outset, the somewhat rural small town atmosphere near my home looked like a perfect match. Because of my own educational experience in a similar sized small town in the Midwest, I knew that the atmosphere would be familiar and comforting. It looked like a fit so far.

I pulled out a thick yellow legal pad for the next step in my analysis. Using the brochure, I focused first on the list of desired professional experiences. On the top of the first page of the legal pad, I listed the first professional qualification desired, "Experience as a superintendent, central office administrator or at least five years as a site principal." Below that description, I listed the related positions I had held as evidence of meeting that first qualification.

On the next page, I wrote the description of professional experience desired: "Experience with an interest-based approach to collaborative bargaining and problem solving." Bingo! I had been a negotiator for several years using an interest-based win-win approach. On page three, I listed: "Experience with district finance and budgeting practices." No problem, I thought, as I listed my experiences with budgets in my years as a principal, coordinator of categorical programs, and committee member on a comprehensive county budget study.

On each page of my legal pad I continued the list of professional and personal descriptions. And below each, I wrote every activity in which I had been involved related to that item. By the end of this ex-

ercise, I had a detailed listing of my experiences and personal qualities as a match for the qualifications listed in the brochure. I saw
many parallels between the district needs and my experiences. But I
needed more data.

I called the city local newspaper and ordered a paper to be delivered
to my home. In the two months prior to the interview I read every issue cover to cover. On another sheet in my legal pad, I began to list the
themes emerging from my reading. Strong support of the schools existed in the community based on the positive headlines about school
programs and activities. Senior citizen involvement in all phases of the
community also seemed to be strong. The athletics programs were of
high interest based on the incredible play-by-play detail in the articles
on the sports pages. There were a large number of photos in each issue
of school related events. All good signs, I thought, of the community's
interest and participation in the school and school events.

The Chamber of Commerce sent me their packet of materials for visitors or individuals inquiring about business opportunities. This information was invaluable in understanding the predominance of family-
owned and small businesses in the community. No major corporations
existed within the district's boundaries. I did discover, however, a large
number of fine and performing arts businesses from the extensive list
of galleries, museums, potters, and graphic design houses. Video pro-
duction facilities, screenwriters and authors were listed as members of
the Chamber. The Chamber documents gave me a sense of the profile
for potential school-business partnerships. It also provided me the
knowledge that visual and performing arts programs in the schools
would be embraced by the business community.

On several weekends I visited the community. After picking up a
map at a local service station, I dotted it with school site locations from
the names and addresses I copied from the public school directory. I
walked around every school site and peeked in classroom windows.
Old schools with aging infrastructures were the norm. I strolled around
the district office and could see that major renovation work was
needed there too. A bond measure for renovation and modernization
seemed like a consideration for this district. At each school, I jotted
down detailed notes of my observations of the warm and inviting environments evident in every classroom despite cracked tiles and anti-
quated lighting fixtures. I counted classrooms and estimated enroll-
ment for each school. Despite the absence of children, I could sense the

culture and climate of the school by looking at the sites. Happily, I discovered many teachers working Saturdays and Sundays, which certainly made a strong statement about professional commitment. Make a note of that too, I thought.

At the city offices, I picked up materials they had about the schools. City staff were very cordial in their offer to call the parks and recreation department to let them know I would be stopping by. At the department, I picked up catalogs of programs offered after school, on weekends and during the summer. I visited the city parks and local sports fields and found them filled with weekend activities. Parents, grandparents, aunts and uncles were watching hundreds of soccer uniformed children.

I visited several real estate offices and asked people about their perceptions of the quality of the local public schools. Office staff and agents enthusiastically shared that people moved to the community due to the quality of the school programs. If there was a problem in the schools, it was directly related to their over-thirty ages of the facilities. "Don't be fooled by the old buildings," I was cautioned, "because we have wonderful programs in the classrooms for our children." The pride in the schools was evident throughout my conversations. However, I did learn of a very real concern about the ability to deliver technology in the aging buildings. I learned that enthusiasm for technology was high among parents, teachers, and students, but often the classrooms couldn't handle the required electrical support for the newest computers. The notes I recorded in detail that evening outlined the need for a long-term strategy for infrastructure improvements to support technological applications.

Visits with students and community members in restaurants and on the street provided me with wonderful anecdotal stories about the teachers, parent involvement, and principal leadership. Many of these stories described touching accounts of support they individually had received or programs that were especially meaningful. I recorded a number of stories I wanted to share at the appropriate time if I were interviewed and later if I got the job.

My appointment with the county superintendent of schools provided in-depth information about the fiscal stability of the district and the documentation I needed that the district had a strong reputation of being well run, efficient, and effective. Alongside the documents the county provided me, I wrote some notes to myself about the county personnel's impression of the integrity of the employees in the school district business office. This validated the professional competence of district staff. To receive more specific detail about the district's budgetary priorities, I called a professional organization that gathers data about financial expenditures for each district in the state. From this data, I gleaned valuable information on district priorities based on spending habits. It was clear that a large investment was made on the instructional program as evidenced by the strong salary schedules and the high proportion of the district budget devoted to personnel. A commitment to top salaries for teachers and support personnel was important. The district was able to attract outstanding professional educators and likely experienced little employee turnover.

A packet of more detailed materials given to me by the district superintendent's office included copies of the school report cards, a directory listing of employees, school newsletters, a report listing student performance data for the past several years, and a brochure about the education foundation.

The existence of an education foundation in the community was a sure sign of support. I knew I could bring ideas and experiences to this foundation from the three foundations I had worked directly with in prior districts. Another match!

After the extensive data gathering, I had numerous yellow legal pads filled with detailed information. I reviewed my notes and continued the process of matching my experiences with the needs listed. My observations and visits provided the detail I needed for the interview process. I was ready!

During my interview, the board members were amazed at the extent of my knowledge about the community. I described their budget priorities in terms of putting instruction for students first. I could sense their looks of, "How did she know that?" When I was asked what concerns I had, I was able to describe in detail the facilities issues I felt would need immediate attention by the new superintendent. I described the challenges presented by thirty-year-old wiring when students needed to be trained using the latest in technology. I commended the board for the phenomenal community support engendered by the schools using touching stories people had shared with me during my visits. I told them that I was pleased the board demonstrated commitment to a high caliber faculty with their support of competitive staff salaries. As I left my final interview, the board thanked me for all the efforts I had made in preparing for the interview. They shared with me that they felt that I knew the community as well as they did. By the time, I got home from the interview, there was a message on my answer machine, "We'd like the new superintendent of our district to call us back as soon as possible so we can make some arrangements for you to join our team."

Not Knowing Your Community Can Backfire

"Without knowing anything about the history of this small community and the many losses, embarrassments and rejections they had felt over the years, what they heard from my wish for a new school was the part about abandoning the old campus."

During my third month as a superintendent, I was excited and proud to be attending the back-to-school nights at all of the schools in my district. I had envisioned myself at these activities many times while preparing for the role of the superintendent. I knew it was important for me to get to as many classrooms as possible during the evening and to sign in on every sign-in sheet. Symbolically it was important for the staff to see the new superintendent on the campus.

Back-to-school night is a ritual most classroom teachers spend considerable time preparing for, and they are usually relieved when it's behind them. However, they appreciate visits to their classrooms by the superintendent and other district office administrators, as it provides them an opportunity to show off their rooms. The more visitors they have, the more appreciated they feel.

The last of the scheduled back-to-school nights in our district was held at the only school in the district outside the city limits. Garfield is a small elementary school with approximately 265 students enrolled in kindergarten through grade five. It is located in a rural area that disincorporated more than 15 years ago during an economic recession when the citizens voted to give up local rule and fall under the jurisdiction of the county government.

Nearly 3,000 people live in this hot, arid, windy location situated south of a major east-west freeway and bounded on the south by mountains and on the north by an Indian reservation of nearly 300 square miles. The remnants of a small two-square-block business district remain and include a post office, general store, county library, and numerous dilapidated, dusty buildings that appeared to be abandoned.

The school is located about two blocks from the main crossroads in town. The main building adjacent to the freeway was constructed in the late 1930s. The other permanent structure is immediately parallel to the original building and was constructed in the 1950s. Four portable classrooms sit to the east on a dirt field.

Other than a small play area designed for kindergartners with a patch of grass located right next to the freeway, there is nothing attractive about this school. When the freeway was constructed in the 1970s the windows on the buildings were boarded up and air conditioners were hung on the walls to minimize freeway noise.

Children walk through the kitchen and pick up their breakfast and lunch and sit outside on old wooden picnic benches placed under an overhang. On the many days when the wind gusts are over fifty miles per hour, sand and dirt blow everywhere. On the rare rainy day, students are faced with the challenge of carrying their food on trays to a classroom where they sit together on the floor in large numbers so they can be supervised inside.

Speech and language services and special testing take place in two small abandoned restrooms. The plumbing remains, although it is not functional. A portable toilet facility was placed on the campus several years ago due to problems with the old septic system. Teachers claim the septic system occasionally gives off fumes that permeate the classrooms.

Most full-time teachers on the campus have been there several years. The kindergarten teacher's wife is the secretary, and their daughter teaches fifth grade. The principal is assigned to another school in town and is only at Garfield on a part-time basis. The staff has learned to be self-sufficient and take care of many problems that would otherwise be handled by an administrator. They work out many problems directly with parents rather than sending children to the office to wait for the principal to handle them.

This description sets the stage for a story that taught me how important it is to know the culture of a community before opening my mouth and making commitments. When I walked on the campus for the Open House, it was my second visit to this school. Lots of cars were parked haphazardly, and more than 100 adults and children were walking around the campus, eating hot dogs and brownies sold by the parents and staff as a fundraiser. Several dogs ran loose and snatched away any food held too carelessly by the smallest children.

I visited every classroom and signed in at each one. As I walked back to the office entrance and greeted the principal, I proclaimed how much I would like to build a new school for these students and their families. It would be a school located far enough away from the freeway and railroad tracks to be safe and have a multipurpose room with a serving kitchen so children could eat inside, away from the wind, sand and rain. It would have grass and be an attractive place where students and staff could be proud of their school and look forward each day to exciting teaching and learning.

As we approached the office I realized everyone around us was listening to our conversation. I willingly repeated my desire for this school to be relocated and replaced in order to provide a safe, adequate and attractive learning environment. When I finished with the details of my "wouldn't it be wonderful if" story, no one responded or asked even one question.

I was not sure what I expected the staff and parents to say, but I recall being somewhat disappointed that no one expressed any enthusiasm or added any ideas of their own. I think I attributed that to politeness and deference to me as the "new" superintendent.

While driving home that night I was determined to find a way to build a new Garfield School. Even though there was absolutely no money on the horizon for such a project, I vowed I would pursue every possible avenue to accomplish this goal. The students, staff and families of this community deserved much more than they had been given.

Imagine my surprise when a week later I was given a copy of a flyer being passed around at Garfield School claiming the new superintendent was planning to close the school and send all of the students to schools in town. Several weeks later at a board meeting four parents of students at Garfield stood up and angrily told how upset they were that their school was going to be closed.

Of course, board members and I denied the rumor and I tried to explain that perhaps the rumor was started by my comments about wanting to build a new school. What a mess I had made! Without knowing anything about the history of this small community and the many losses, embarrassments and rejections they had felt over the years, what they heard from my wish for a new school was the part about abandoning the old campus. What they heard was a threat, not a promise.

What a lesson I learned about the need to become familiar with the history and culture of an existing community! Even today, as the new Garfield School is being constructed, there are staff and community members remembering a string of broken promises who say they won't believe it is true until they move in.

THERE IS NO "ONE" COMMUNITY

"By knowing me, community members might be more likely to call me if they had future questions or heard something that disturbed them. And, they might be more likely to offer ideas to help create understanding."

Each school district has its own identity. A small school district may have only one community with similar types of people. A larger school district may cover many communities with diverse populations. In either case the superintendent must be aware that communities are always changing.

As districts experience significant growth and demographic changes, issues evolve from unexpected sources and the potential for dissension surfaces. In changing times, the superintendent's challenge is to establish an atmosphere of cooperation and interdependence, embracing differences and encouraging an open forum for problem solving.

In any one district, there are multiple constituencies, even multiple communities. The effective leader knows change is inevitable and a sign of a dynamic organization, requiring flexibility.

The community you meet with regarding an issue today will not be the same community in three years. Parents with students moving through your schools now may be different from parents of the entering students in a few years. You must meet with the community on an on-going basis or risk losing touch with the changing community, one with no knowledge or memory of the history of the district.

Communities Are Always Changing

As a result of rampant growth, our district planned for multi-track, year-round education as a way to accommodate students while we were building schools.

We held meetings throughout the district, and took community input. Then we developed a plan to implement a multi-track, year-round schedule at one school. A second school would convert to multi-track, year-round two years later.

Plans went as scheduled until it was necessary to place a third school on a multi-track, year-round schedule. Because we had not continued to meet with the parents of the third school, they were not aware of the plan to have their school go on a multi-track, year-round schedule.

The community was angry and upset that they did not have input into the decision. In fact, they were right. The parents who had been there in the beginning of the conversion to year-round were part of the decision, but the parents who moved into the community since that time were not. District leaders had not continued meetings to address ongoing facility needs and to include parents in continuing plans for multi-track, year-round schedules.

By not being aware the community had changed, even though the demographics had not, and not maintaining open, on-going communication, we created a confrontational situation we could have avoided.

Channeling the Energy of Special Interest Groups

> "The dilemma was how to acknowledge their legitimate concerns, put to rest their unfounded concerns, and at the same time, not pull the rug out from under our staff and the efforts they were making to implement the program."

During my first year as superintendent, we piloted a math series and ultimately adopted it. I admit that during that time I paid little attention to the adoption process since there were three other tumultuous issues taking my attention. In retrospect, I wish I had been more involved.

In reality not all teachers were supportive of the new text and their concerns were being conveyed to parents. One particular group of parents who had followed the math text controversy throughout the state, formed into an organized force to raise parental concerns that this "new math" was going to seriously harm students. The group, made up primarily of five men, a few with engineering backgrounds, used the Internet to gain information and patterned themselves after a group in another part of the state. Luckily, I knew the superintendent in another district where this issue had arisen, and he gave me some good insights and ideas.

One of the first things I did was to bring this special interest group together with staff and board members so we could hear their concerns. We met a couple times to try to resolve their issues. While I did not like their approach, which was often aggressive and attacking in nature, I recognized they had some valid points. The dilemma was how to acknowledge their legitimate concerns, put to rest their unfounded fears, and at the same time, not pull the rug out from under our staff and the efforts they were making to implement the program.

At first, the members of the group were able to generate support and people attended board meetings to voice their opinions. Teachers who were supportive of the program were put on the defensive. Teachers not supportive of the program formed an allegiance with the group but did not want to put their colleagues in a difficult position.

I tried to do several things to resolve the situation. Some of them worked well, while others were not so helpful. By bringing the special interest group into discussions with staff, I gave them a voice and acknowledged legitimate points. I was also able to also show them that some of their arguments about the texts were not valid.

One of the biggest lessons for me was that by bringing a special interest group into the discussion and making them part of the resolution, we diffused most of the animosity. It seemed in retrospect that they wanted a fight, which was something I refused to do.

Attempting to Bring the Community Together

"I tried to help people see each other as real people with different points of view and not as evil persons."

When the election no one expected happened, the philosophical position of the Board of Education majority turned abruptly to the right. The new majority, made up of religious conservatives, began to dominate the agenda.

Facts, opinions, and rumors about what "they" were doing, or might do, became the common topic of conversation. Facts and misinformation were rampant not only in the broader community, but within the various faith communities as well, with people turning to their particular religious leaders for "the truth."

As superintendent, I spent considerable time calming fears, explaining board actions, and separating fact from fiction. I tried to help people see each other as real people with different points of view and not as evil persons. It meant walking a tightrope between reassuring people that everything would be okay and dealing with the reality that a major philosophical shift on the governing board had occurred, with the outcome unknown.

Nonetheless, the general atmosphere became one of suspicion both within the district and across the community. Trust diminished, fear increased and the time and attention of the staff shifted from established district goals to dealing with perceived and actual threats to the very mission of the district.

Troubling to me was the increasing suspicion of school district staff by the leaders and members of the various Christian faiths. I was also deeply concerned about the growing fragmentation and open hostility around virtually every issue. People took sides and quickly became entrenched. My thinking became focused on what I could do in a proactive way to promote communication and understanding between all board members and people across the political and philosophical spectrum.

My beginning step was to hold a series of breakfast discussions with the leaders of the faith communities represented in the district. These included the Protestant and Evangelical churches which predominated the community, and also Catholic, Bahai, Buddhist, Jewish and nondenominational faith communities. When I received a call from a person wanting to know if atheists were invited, I said "Of course," and she joined the discussion.

I had several goals for these breakfast meetings. First was to have a low-key, informal gathering to put a "face" on the district. People are more likely to ask for information or check out a rumor if we are "real" people to each other, and we understand each other's values. The second purpose was an exchange of accurate information. It was critical that I clearly articulate the district's mission, goals, and values as well as our position on a variety of issues of interest to these religious leaders. Of major value was clearing up misunderstandings about the public schools' relationship to religion and how we do and can work together, capitalizing on our unique and complimentary roles and responsibilities. We broke down the myth that public schools are hostile to religion. A third goal was to determine the level of support for an idea I was formulating, that of creating a Common Ground Task Force (CGTF). The CGTF would be made up of leaders/ representatives of all the faith communities within our district boundaries. We would create a forum for civil conversation among people of good will and strong beliefs, develop a common understanding of the role of religion in the schools, and develop agreements about basic values to guide the board and district regarding policy decisions.

The opinions of individuals and groups would be solicited, discussed, and honored. The CGTF would work for consensus on common beliefs that people throughout the community could support. Rather than focusing on the disagreements as the pattern had developed, we would work to discover those areas where we had agreement. Often people find many areas where they don't really disagree when they meet face to face and discuss their views. Frequently the disagreements are perceptual, the result of misinformation or miscommunication.

At a large meeting of all those who had been invited to the smaller meetings, I asked, "Would you give your time and energy to talk about common values that could provide guidance for the district?" Without exception, these leaders said "Yes!" All along I kept the board members informed of who attended each breakfast and the topics discussed. I told them of the idea of a CGTF, the reasoning behind it, and the growing support among the religious leaders. Each board member thought the meetings were a good idea, but the board majority was apprehensive about the CGTF. Long before the CGTF proposal came to the board for discussion at a public board meeting for discussion only, I sent them drafts. I met individually with each member, offering my view that the Task Force would reduce tension, build support for a number of their philosophies, and would result in a positive statement of leadership by this board.

The interest across the community and in the media was astounding. Resumes and letters of interest came to my office from people with amazing and diverse backgrounds, expressing their interest in being part of the CGTF, to heal and help the district progress. Newspaper articles and editorials supported the idea. Unfortunately, the board majority was not persuaded and the recommendation to create a CGTF was defeated on a 3–2 vote. Very telling were statements made by members of the majority at the meeting, who indicated they, and only they, were the decision-makers. One stated, "We are the community; we will decide."

Despite the board's rejection, and the loss I felt, I believed the effort was correct and valuable for the community, the staff and for my peace of mind. My belief was a continued confirmation from people throughout the community by their expressions of disappointment and commitment to try to move forward. I was particularly moved by the response from the faith community leaders. Their calls and letters convinced me that while the CGTF was defeated, the goals of the breakfast meetings had been achieved. Many of these faith community leaders, even those located within blocks of each other, had never met and they thanked me for bringing them together. Others said they felt better about the public schools and saw ways we could work together. They indicated it was time to start an interfaith council, and pledged their support for the efforts to bring people together.

I believed that despite the board's rejection of this effort to bring calm and reason to a troubled district, there would be a positive outcome. A lesson I learned was that even in difficult times, as a leader, you can make positive things happen when you stay true to your basic values. Keeping your focus on what truly matters is essential. Sometimes, you will figure out an approach that is positive for the school community and the community at large—one you might not have thought of in smoother, more "normal" times.

Rising to Community Expectations: Fire at the Middle School

> "The major factor that influenced my decision was considering what the families of the students and the community would expect us to do."

In November of 1993 Southern California experienced numerous large wildfires that burned out of control for days at a time. A wildfire of unknown origin started in our community and burned thousands of acres over a five-day period. Santa Ana winds blew throughout this period at more than fifty miles per hour and temperatures soared into the nineties and higher.

The fire was discovered about 10:00 a.m. in the underdeveloped foothills at the end of a residential street four blocks from Highland Middle School. While administrators in the district were meeting at a regular monthly Leadership Team meeting, the principal of Highland was called to the telephone. She returned hastily and announced she had to leave because of a wildfire near her school.

I immediately adjourned the meeting and followed the principal to her school. Several police cars and fire trucks were at the school when we arrived. We walked to the upper play field of the campus, seeing columns of smoke and flames moving parallel to the school in the foothills.

A few minutes after my phone request, a police lieutenant came to the school to brief us on the status of the fire. He told us that at this stage, the fire was unpredictable, but that the school was probably not in danger.

After another trip to the upper campus it was evident the wind was mounting and so was the fire. I called the principal, vice principal, counselor, and office staff together and told them that even though the police department believed the school and the nearly 1,100 students and staff were safe, we were evacuating the campus.

The major factor influencing my decision was grave concern for the students and their families. As educators the legal term *in loco parentis* is powerful; we act on behalf of the parents. This situation seemed to magnify that responsibility many times over. The entire community expects us to be the guardians and protectors of the children.

With the decision made, we assigned duties and within twenty minutes, we had relocated the students and staff to the high school gymnasium two miles away. After ensuring everyone understood what they were to do, I directed traffic in front of the school while buses arrived to carry students to safety. Family members drove frantically down the street looking at the smoke and fire and asking where we had taken their children.

At the gymnasium we set up a check-out table using student emergency cards to keep track of students we released to parents. We brought in lunch and started a student-faculty volleyball tournament. Nearly fifty percent of the students were picked up before the day was over.

Although the fire expanded, it moved west and ultimately did not threaten the school. For weeks after the fire we heard from families and community members how pleased they were we had taken such aggressive action to protect their students; it affirmed that our actions matched the values of our community.

DEVELOPING COMMUNITY RELATIONSHIPS

Removing Barriers to Serve Families

"A superintendent can make an enormous difference in the lives of people by removing institutional barriers that traditionally block collaborative efforts."

The high number of needy families was almost overwhelming when I arrived as superintendent in a new district. Forty percent of the families with children enrolled in school were receiving some form of welfare assistance, and nearly eighty percent of all the students were eligible to receive free or reduced-cost lunches. As I got to know the community, it also became apparent that existing resources were confusing to access and services to families were fragmented.

Within three months, I started inviting community leaders and service providers to come together on a bimonthly basis to identify the highest priority of unmet needs of students and their families and to seek ways to address those needs. During the first two years, we gathered data from such sources as County Public Health, Child Protective Services, and United Way agencies, and continued to expand the circle of people who attended our meetings. We discussed issues and concerns and educated each other about the functions, responsibilities, and language of each agency.

By the end of the second year we chose teen pregnancy prevention and services to teens with babies as our highest priorities. We sat with laptop computers and, as we wrote a Teen Pregnancy Prevention grant application, we built relationships. When the grant was not funded we refused to be discouraged. We went on to write a Healthy Start Program application. It was not funded. We then wrote a California Wellness Foundation application, which was also not funded.

Undaunted, we submitted a Family Preservation and Support application to the Department of Social Services. We were ecstatic when it was funded for three years! It was our first success. This project brought an infant care center to the high school campus and allowed teen mothers who had dropped out due to lack of childcare to come back to school. It also allowed us to start classes addressing issues such as parenting for males, resisting drug and alcohol abuse, building self-esteem and developing career interests. Eleven agencies were involved in this collaboration.

By the fall of our third year, we celebrated the grand opening of the Family Connections office located in a bank building on Main Street, right in front of a very convenient bus stop. This was funded by a Healthy Start grant. The mayor, legislative representatives, business and community leaders, school district staff, students and families joined agency representatives at this gala event. During the celebration of speeches, presentations and certificates of appreciation, the telephone rang several times with offers for help. These calls were gratifying because it was evident to all that Family Connections was already making a difference in the community.

The benefits to students and their families derived from this project were incalculable. While I had some initial concerns about the time I spent in meetings with representatives from social service agencies and other local agencies such as the hospital, YMCA, recreational leaders, and other community agencies, the outcome of this collaboration convinced me the time invested was more valuable than I ever imagined.

The lesson learned from this small project is that a superintendent can make an enormous difference in the lives of people by removing institutional barriers that traditionally block collaborative efforts on behalf of our students and their families. While collaboration is a lengthy, tedious and involved process, the successful superintendent knows it is absolutely essential. Our collective conversations clearly evolved around the familiar adage "the sum is greater than the individual parts." Communities working collaboratively make differences in the lives of its children, and together even the most challenging obstacles can be overcome.

Don't Forget the "Ordinary People"

> "Parents and grandparents are always among our Ordinary People but we also have neighbors, friends, pets, and teachers."

Ordinary people. What is so special about them? They make the world go around, yet we forget about them most of the time.

To acknowledge our ordinary people, every few years we have an Ordinary People Contest in our district. Students in all grade levels

and at all sites write an essay about a person who has made a difference in their lives. Even the kindergartners contribute. They dictate
their stories and either an older student or an adult writes them down.
All the stories are reviewed, and a winner is selected at each grade
level. All of the essays, selected and not selected, are put into a book.
The books are distributed to each site and district office for others to
read and enjoy.

At a celebration, each student reads his/her essay out loud and
presents an award to his/her "Ordinary Person." As you listen to the
stories being read, some make you laugh and others bring tears to
your eyes. One story was written by a fourth grader who had her
grandmother accept the award for her grandfather who had recently
died. The sixth grader shared his thoughts about his younger sister
who was ill with cancer. When a third grader described how a friend
was there for him when he was in the hospital, the audience was taking out their tissues.

This evening is one of the most uplifting and emotional held in our
community. Parents and grandparents are usually among our Ordinary
People, but we also have neighbors, friends, pets and teachers
awarded. Each person is special because a child's life was touched in a
special way by these "Ordinary People."

Living Treasures

> "It's a grass roots process that selects individuals with integrity
> who are willing to share their expertise with the community they
> love."

Ordinary people often do extraordinary things. I discovered a wonderful organization developed by one simple, ordinary senior citizen
who realized he was surrounded by some very interesting people in his
community who had a lot to offer. This organization is dedicated to recognizing people in the area who contribute to the community. These individuals take their unique talents and skills and begin programs that
continue their good work.

As the education representative on the Board of Directors of this organization, I have learned what an impact a simple idea has on the
lives of our youth. Many of the individuals recognized were not part of
an organized community group with whom I would have typically
had contact. One spring weekend dozens of residents gathered in a

beautiful home overlooking our valley. The group was celebrating this year's special group of individuals . . . our community's recently chosen "Living Treasures." "It's a grass roots process that selects individuals with integrity who are willing to share their expertise with the community they love," the founder shared with newly selected local Living Treasures. Many of the individuals recognized had projects focused on helping youth.

The organization now boasts well over 100 individuals identified as the community's "Living Treasures." The special group chosen that year included a teacher who supports positive self-images among our youth, the assistant superintendent of the public school system who coordinates a summer hospice camp for grieving families, and a recording artist who shares his legends and dance skills to celebrate Latin American culture. They were joined by a bank vice president, who doubles as a weekend captain of a swift water rescue team and who planned to educate the community about safety and the dangers of swift water. Also included is the executive director of the community's youth foundation who developed a web page to keep the entire community informed about the exciting programs available for the youth and adult residents in the community.

From one ordinary senior citizen with an extraordinary idea came a dynamic team of well over 100 individuals who give enormous amounts of their time, talent and love to the community.

Seniors for Schools: An Invaluable Resource

"Educators often comment on the vast untapped resource of the senior population, but rarely do they aggressively pursue their participation in our schools."

After I read the job posting for the superintendency, I began the process of researching community perceptions of the eight schools in the 4,000-student district. Many of the accolades I heard about the community came from senior citizens I met on the street during my visits, or those I read about in the local newspaper to which I had subscribed.

Educators often comment on the vast untapped resource of the senior population, but rarely do they aggressively pursue their participation in our schools. The occasional classroom senior volunteer, guest speaker, or grandparent visit is often the extent of classroom involvement.

This community quickly proved to me that seniors were far from passive, occasional participants in community events and in the classrooms of the district. The senior population is one of the most dynamic in town! Considered somewhat of a retirement community, this city exudes an enthusiasm for its senior residents. Seniors are active throughout the city, and their talents and expertise are embraced.

Most local community organizations have large numbers of senior board members. The local jazz, art, quilt, and holiday celebrations are led by senior citizens. Vans buzz around the city driven by senior volunteers who transport older seniors to health appointments, leisure activities, and volunteer placements. A recent library funding initiative was successful in large part due to the efforts of an intense group of committed senior citizens. Classrooms are filled with seniors grading papers, coaching youngsters in mathematics, or listening to beginning readers huddled in a corner. I am continually amazed at the numbers of seniors who believe so passionately in their roles as surrogate parents that they wouldn't dream of missing a day of their commitment. Students look wide-eyed as the door swings open and the seniors walk in. Teachers and principals are pleased and proud to have their assistance and wisdom.

Over five hundred community volunteers gather at an annual culminating picnic each spring when they are honored for the tens of thousands of hours of volunteer time they give to every organization in our valley. It is a joyous sight! Beyond the certificates, plaques, and ribbons are the intangible rewards felt by the seniors. Those who volunteer in the schools are blessed with daily hugs from children and bushels of gratitude from teachers for their gifts of time.

Not surprising to me was the recent leadership of a retired teacher and former big-city union steward in a bond measure for renovation and modernization of our school sites. Pegged as "Seniors for Schools!" the team assumed complete responsibility for registering new senior voters and assuring that absentee ballots were requested and properly completed by those unable to travel to the polls. A speaker's bureau was formed to visit trailer parks, nursing homes, and adult day care centers to address the positive impact of the measure on property values and the local economy. Phone banks were filled with senior volunteers in the evenings as community residents were called with bond measure information. During the two weekends prior to the election, precincts were visited with senior walkers delivering literature. Testimonials were printed in the local papers, and literature listing supportive senior community leaders was distributed to service clubs, churches, and businesses.

The successful passage of this measure can be attributed largely to the caring, concern, and commitment demonstrated by a dynamic group of retirees. Superintendents who fail to embrace and engage the talents of the senior population in their communities are missing something very special. The memories our students will have because of the seniors in their daily lives will hopefully imbue them with the same volunteer spirit as they grow older. The wisdom shared and the energy exhibited by our Seniors for Schools! has been a source of great inspiration to an already optimistic community of educators and residents.

Service Club Partnerships: A Gold Mine of Support

"Service clubs [are] among the most valuable assets. . . . [They] are just waiting to be included in the plans for reaching the goals of the district."

"We couldn't do it without you!" is a familiar statement from school leaders who are blessed with strong partnerships with community service organizations. Almost every organization from Rotary International, Kiwanis, and the Optimists to Friends of the Library, Lions, and the Chamber of Commerce has a section of its mission statement focused on service to youth. As I take a new administrative position in a community, one of the first checks I make is on the extent of involvement of local service organizations in the schools. In every case, I have found service clubs among the most valuable assets in the community. Often, the members are just waiting to be included in the plans for reaching the goals of the district.

From the often-repeated statement, "It takes a village . . ." we are reminded of the power of community. High-performing school districts have long recognized the significant impact that can be made with community outreach programs. The benefits are numerous. Student-business mentorships, scholarships from professional organizations for students pursuing a specific field of endeavor, recognition of community service with savings bonds, and athletic program enhancements are but a very few of the phenomenal benefits for our schools. The creativity and possibilities are endless for service club involvement.

In our small community, a renowned "Tri Tip Sandwich" booth hosted by a senior service club at Friday night football games is as much part of the culture as the game itself. It's the best meal in town on the weekend! The proceeds go directly into our outstanding athletic program. More importantly, the club's visible presence affords them a steady stream of new members from generation to generation. Fathers and sons join together and contribute their time and service, side by side.

Career Weeks, exposing students to future work opportunities and local business mentors who take students "under their wings," solidify a commitment to the economic success of our youth. Regional Occupational Programs, in partnership with community organizations, provide enhanced job opportunities and instructional support materials for students pursuing careers. Retired senior volunteer organizations are thrilled to support literacy programs when asked. Rarely will you ever find an organization unwilling to help purchase uniforms for choral music and band programs. Student performances are given at service club events, and sincere thank-you letters from principals and teachers are read aloud at every meeting. As members hear the appreciation expressed in these letters, commitment to the next project begins!

Service clubs are always looking for speakers for the weekly or monthly meetings. After researching the variety of service clubs in a community, I enthusiastically volunteered to be a speaker early on in my tenure in a new position. This willingness to address a wide range of groups has given me immediate access to an important group of community leaders. It also provided a forum to express my vision for excellence in the school district. Through early and regular visits, speaking engagements and membership in service groups, I have validated with my presence my belief that service groups' participation with us in the education of our youth is essential.

To meet our challenges, we need to reach out to every constituent group in the community to help our youth succeed. "We can't do it without you!" needs to be a message administrators model by their participation with, and involvement in, local service clubs. What an opportunity we have if we reach out with this simple message!

Partnering for Win-Win Outcomes

"That relationship with the Director of Development Services and his staff has paid off in many ways."

We have a positive relationship with our city government and the staff, but it is not without tensions. Two new housing developments were in the planning stages at the time I assumed my job, and I was thrust into a negotiating role I had not anticipated nor experienced.

I was thrust into this situation with the district's lawyer, the city's development services department, a district consultant for a fee study, and two developers and their consultants. One developer was trying to work with us to achieve a satisfactory mitigation agreement, while the other seemed to want to pay as little as possible to mitigate the development's impacts on our schools.

The Director of Development Services was a member of my service club and, coincidentally, shared my birthday. He took time to help me understand the city's approval process. He worked with our consultants, with the developers' representatives, and with me to ensure mitigation agreements were in place prior to city approval of the specific plans.

We were able to reach a satisfactory agreement with one developer, but not with the other. The second developer simply stopped meeting with us. When it came time for specific plan approval, this second developer was, in fact, assessed mitigation fees by the city in excess of the first developer. The city needed to be assured the district would receive appropriate financial compensation for the impacts on our facilities.

I was sitting at the city council meeting when action was taken. The developer seemed amazed, but our attorney and I were delighted!

The relationship with the Director of Development Services and his staff has paid off in many ways. As we have continued our plans for building a new school in one of the developments, the landowner changed. The new owner was difficult to deal with, and the project was delayed. However, because of the previous relationship established with the Development Services Department, we were able to reach satisfactory agreements with the city's full cooperation.

THE MEDIA IS THE COMMUNITY, TOO

Media Relations as Art, Not Science

"A wise superintendent embraces the media by providing extensive information and support to the press on an ongoing basis."

Every superintendent hopes, wishes, or believes that every media depiction of the school district will be accurate, newsworthy and positive.

This dream often goes unrealized, as indicated when I read the daily morning newspaper or watch the local evening television news shows. As a superintendent, my worst nightmare is that the community will perceive our schools as unsafe places for young people or view our staff as unable to protect students in the event of a disaster. With this concern, as well as the memory of media blunders in my early days as a new superintendent, I now have our leadership team plan our media strategy as carefully as we develop our disaster plan. We hope we will not be placed in the position of having to use the section labeled "Responding to a Crisis."

Our media relations planning received an even sharper focus after an incident when my bad dream became a reality. It was an unseasonably warm day in April. About 11 a.m., I was informed that the hills across the street from one of our elementary schools were burning and the smoke was so intense we might need to evacuate the school. Our transportation department was notified and buses were dispatched to the school. A half hour later, a call came from a district administrator warning me the winds had caused the fire to jump a major traffic artery in our community and the fire was heading toward the high school. I called a nearby middle school and told the principal to be ready to receive 2,000 high school students. Following this call, the high school principal made the decision to evacuate. Since the fire threatening the elementary school had shifted course and it was out of danger, the buses originally dispatched to this site were redirected to the high school. The third call from the high school brought news that there was only one passable route from the district office to the high school. On my way to the high school, I drove by three elementary schools that could be in the path of one of the three fires burning in the community that day. However, as was the case with the first fire, the winds shifted the fires over the hills, fortunately away from these sites.

When I arrived at the high school, I could not believe my eyes. Two news helicopters were circling overhead, cars were pouring out of the student parking lot, and students were walking down the street heading toward their homes because they refused to ride the buses sent to evacuate them to the middle school. Law enforcement and fire personnel were everywhere. Staff members were either directing students across the parking lot to buses or directing traffic out of the student parking lot. A deputy sheriff told me he had heard that special education students in wheelchairs were still inside the building. I confirmed he was in error because they had been evacuated first. It was the blackest and heaviest smoke I had ever encountered. As I walked across the parking lot, someone pointed me out as the superintendent. Three television news microphones were thrust in my face. One reporter asked if I was pleased about the way the staff was handling things. Knowing I did not have a complete picture of the situation, I said something about being pleased about the way things were being handled. When the situation on the high school campus seemed to be under control, I drove to the middle school evacuation site. Staff had been involved in an all-day, in-service program, so no students were present. The middle school was able to accommodate the high school students without disruption. Several of us stayed in the parking lot to talk to high school parents who had been directed to the middle school for normal after-school pickups. After the last bus left the parking lot, images of what might be on television that evening flashed through my mind.

As I sat watching the evening news coverage of local events, I saw a camera shot of the blackened 39-acre field where the fire had come right to the edge of the fence at the high school earlier in the day. This relatively calm picture gave little hint to the mad scramble for safety from the intense black smoke, cinders, and heat encountered by our students and staff just a few hours earlier. The next sound bite came from two high school male students who were interviewed at the now famous (at least in our community) "Welcome Market". Their comments included statements such as: "teachers were banging on kids' cars," "people were panicking and running everywhere," "we didn't want to leave our cars there," and "it was a mess." My immediate observation to my husband was, of all of the people to interview and place on the evening news, why did they select the piece featuring the Welcome Market boys? I mentioned that they were truant since they were on television rather than at the evacuation site. A few minutes later, I received a call from my board president who remarked, "I thought you said things went well out there." I carefully explained to her the media had dozens of opportunities to show a different side of the day's events and if we both had been watching another channel, another picture might have emerged. We talked about how they selected the Welcome Market boys. She was reassured when I told her the principal would send a letter to parents explaining the day's events and describing any future changes the school would make in the unlikely event we would ever need to evacuate the school again. She seemed satisfied, but I knew that this was not the end of the story.

In the days following the fire, my assumptions were confirmed. A number of staff and community members watched other local news stations and told me they had seen me walking through the smoke-filled school parking lot and being interviewed by the media. Their impression was that I appeared in charge and had very little time for frivolous media questions. However, I also encountered those who had viewed the Welcome Market segment. I found myself having to talk about the day at the PTA Council meeting, the Chamber of Commerce Board meeting, and my local Rotary Club. Since we often discussed the media's coverage of our community, they were sympathetic and let the matter drop.

This particular media event prompted us to examine our board policy on media access to our schools. It also resulted in my decision to hold yet another meeting with our principals to discuss their responsibility in taking charge when media representatives are on campus, especially in the event of a crisis or disaster. We recognized any story involving students' safety had great potential for being sensationalized and we needed to have a carefully crafted strategy for giving the media accurate information. The new policy directs staff to require all media representatives check in at the school office. This policy ensures that students' and staff safety and privacy will not be compromised and that the educational program will be minimally impacted. The policy also designated a media area for staff to provide accurate information about the situation and the actions being taken to ensure the safety and security of all. Following the adoption of our new media access policy, a reporter challenged me after a board meeting and noted if he wanted to go anywhere on any campus there was not "a damn thing" that I could do about it. I responded he may be correct, but I would hope he would respect our policy for the safety of students. I addressed the need to have good management practices in place and this was a part of any responsible management plan. When he did not entirely accept my rationale, I decided to give him a concrete example. I described the events surrounding the fire, and he remarked, "So you are saying it was a media circus." I did not confirm his remarks and he dropped that line of questioning. Nonetheless, his story about our new policy was balanced, and it also contained my measured response.

From time to time, during our district-wide disaster drills, the district director of disaster preparedness writes a scenario involving the media so school principals have an opportunity to practice our media relations strategy. Our motto is, "Be proactive with the media rather than reactive; you will lose less sleep."

In any community, the media loves to publish news about the fears, trepidation and missteps of school leaders. In order to minimize the impacts of "roller coaster" reporting, a wise superintendent embraces the media by providing extensive information and support to the press on an ongoing basis and institutes a clear and unambiguous media policy.

The Long Walk to the Morning Paper

"The print media has a powerful influence in the life of a super-intendent."

Sometime in his or her career, every superintendent faces the "long walk to the morning newspaper" no matter how long the driveway actually is. The print media has a powerful influence in the life of a superintendent because a newspaper is a distributed communication among community members who typically do not have children in school.

For several years, I lived in a house with a long driveway and each morning at 6:00 a.m. I would make the long walk to pick up the newspaper. During particularly tumultuous time of contentious labor negotiations and dealing with a new board member whose agenda was "my head on a platter," it dawned on me how tense I was each morning when I walked down the driveway to pick up the daily newspaper. My stomach and my shoulders would knot up, and I would hold my breath as I slipped the rubber band off the paper and scanned the headlines while returning to the house. I always hoped the headlines said nothing controversial or negative about me or anyone else in my school district. I realized I also hoped that no one else in public education was being beaten up either.

Early on in my career I heard at a public relations workshop that it takes ten positive articles to overcome one negative one. I had learned over the years that the inexperienced and young journalists were often assigned to the education beat. They looked for the controversial and negative articles that could grab the headlines and attention so they could be promoted to more prestigious assignments. In spite of my efforts to put forward ideas about positive things happening at schools in classrooms, many of the reporters I worked with considered these to be "feel good" stories and neither they, nor their editors, were interested. What they wanted was something with more "meat."

As superintendent, I believed it was important to let the community know what we were doing in schools. Since nearly three quarters of the community members did not have school-age children, the local newspaper was one of the few ways I could communicate with them. Each month I would call the local education reporter and suggest several topics he or she might want to write about. I would offer to draft the story and to give her contacts at the schools.

Unfortunately, for several years I had the experience of working with a young woman who was absolutely uninterested in any of my story ideas. Instead, she focused on contentious issues that existed in the community about the schools or the district. She would only call me about a story after collecting comments and opinions from as many people as possible. She would call to ask for single line quote from me before the story went to press. These unbalanced stories appeared regularly, and I had no venue to respond or provide another point of view to the community. I certainly learned about the power of the press. This was a very frustrating time and it made those walks down the driveway each morning longer and longer.

When the Media Calls

> "Being firm and stating parameters is essential not only for the superintendent, but . . . to protect everyone in the district."

Some topics are sure to produce media attention. Biggies are the evolution-creationism debate, sex education, educating illegal immigrants, turning down or accepting large government grants, hiring attorneys with specific philosophical biases, etc. When all of these things happen in one district in a short period of time, you can expect intense media attention. Suddenly the question of what to do when *60 Minutes* shows up on your doorstep takes on new meaning.

Our district faced all of these issues within a few months. For districts with a public relations person, working with the media is a simpler task. However, most districts, ours included, did not have that luxury. We gathered materials from various workshops on working with the media and held planning sessions about how to effectively respond to the media and who would be the spokesperson on each issue. It was up to us.

The assistant superintendents and I were the central brainstorming and planning group. Our first order of business was to clarify, in straightforward language, exactly what our positions and recommendations would be for presentation to the board. After board meetings, we needed to be able to state clearly and succinctly, both verbally and in writing, the actions taken by the board.

Strong media relations are always important, but in times of turmoil, quick and clear statements are critical. Our district was covered by large and small, local and national newspapers with reporters of varying experience and skill. We consciously worked to give equal time to all of them. This was more important than it may have seemed on the surface. The national media has a broader audience, but the local reporters covered us before and will long after the crisis time is over. Ultimately the local media have far more power to help or hurt the long-term efforts and image of the district.

I learned to be cautious and judicious in what I said while being as open as possible and responding to each media person with promptness, kindness, understanding, and respect. I also learned quickly that respect is not a part of the behavior of all media people. In one case, a television reporter and cameraman walked into my office, demanding to see me. I went nose to nose with her and in a very soft voice told her she would never get another story if she did not go back to the outer office and ask my assistant in a respectful way when I would be available. When she started to argue, I simply asked her what she didn't understand about my statement to her.

She apologized and did as requested. I met with her ten minutes later and was responsive and respectful. At the end of our conversation, the reporter apologized and said she had been afraid she wouldn't meet her deadline. I told her I would always try to assist her, but only when she behaved respectfully to everyone in the organization. Being firm and stating parameters is essential not only as appropriate behavior for the superintendent, but to provide a model and to protect everyone in the district.

Perhaps the most important lesson of all is to never speak with the media regarding the intentions of others. Speak only about the actions of the board. When reporters would ask me why the board, or certain members of the board, voted as they did, I always referred them back to those board members. I made it clear I would speak about the actions the board took and how the staff and I would carry out their directives, but never about the intent of the board. A standard response was "None of us knows what is in the hearts and minds of others. To learn that, you will have to speak the individuals themselves." Remember, the reporter wants a headline; don't let it to be you.

LESSONS LEARNED

- Read the local papers before you join a new district.
- Observe, listen, and record what you learn about the community from various sources.
- Learn the history and culture of the district before attempting change.
- Participate in local organizations; it demonstrates you care about the community.
- Inspire others to become involved in community service.
- Remember, the community expects you to be the guardian of all its children.
- Call on and count on the network of community support for the schools during both positive and challenging times.
- Withhold final judgment while you listen with an open mind to all sides.
- Encourage participation of community groups with differing perspectives.
- Demonstrate the entire community's concern about the welfare of its youth through relationships with other organizations and agencies.
- Create collaborative efforts to remove institutional barriers to help students and families.
- Collaborate for personal and professional growth; you are less effective in isolation.
- Seek out and acknowledge ordinary heroes of all ages.
- Have a media relations policy and action plan.
- Bring critics into the discussion and make them part of the solution.
- Give the district a human face in the community by being part of the community.
- Successes can emerge out of apparent failures.

Chapter 2

Knowing Your Board

"While the board acts as one body in a public meeting, board members are clearly unique individuals with their own goals and beliefs about education. Boards and superintendents who treat each other with respect and have common goals for students demonstrate to the community a true sense of teamwork."

Relationships are the key to success—and survival. You hear it over and over. For the superintendent, the relationship with the board of education is absolutely critical to your success and tenure in the job. The highs, lows, twists and turns of the job are often determined by interactions with board members.

From the beginning, it is important to define how best to communicate with the board as a whole and with each individual board member. While the board acts as one body in a public meeting, board members are clearly unique individuals with their own goals and beliefs about education. How the superintendent acknowledges those individuals' strengths and needs sends a message to the community.

Boards and superintendents who treat each other with respect and have common goals for students demonstrate to the community a true sense of teamwork. We are all in this together to create exciting results, and we must commit to staying together through the rough spots. When contentious relationships and behavior are evident, confidence in the system is diminished within the community.

Examining what superintendents do and how they work with their boards of education tells us much about how to survive, and thrive, in this challenging role.

YOUR BOARD IS YOUR BOSS

"Quality businesses have owners who take pride in quality leadership, management, and products. The customer feels satisfied and pleased when you appreciate the people who work in the business."

School districts are owned by the community. This community ownership is represented by elected board members. The success (and length of service) of the chief executive officer, the superintendent, is often determined by the quality and commitment to success of these representatives of the local owners—the school board.

Who the owners are, what they care about, and how the superintendent interacts with them can make the journey smooth or bumpy, long or short. Board membership changes can also impact the way the superintendent works and how effectively the district operates.

Bossy, Bossy

"Children can get to the heart of a matter and state the critical issues with uncanny insight."

One afternoon, my deputy superintendent picked up his second-grade daughter after school. As they drove out of the school parking lot, the dad waved at a woman driving past. Always curious, daughter Hillary asked, "Who was that, Dad?" "That's Mrs. Carter, she's a school board member," he replied. "What's that mean? What does a school board member do?" Hillary asked. "Well, she's one of the superintendent's bosses," he explained. "You know, just like the superintendent's my boss, Mrs. Carter is one of her bosses."

Hillary looked at him skeptically. "What do you mean *one* of her bosses?" Dad replied that the superintendent's boss was the school board that had five people on it. One of these five was Mrs. Carter. Now, Hillary knew her dad was quite a kidder, and a great storyteller. Her response to his explanation was one of disbelief. "Nuh-uh, Dad!"

she said. "You only have the superintendent as your boss, so she can't have five bosses. Everyone has only one boss."

"Hillary, I'm telling you the truth. The superintendent has these five bosses who make up the school board." "Nuh-uh!" No matter how hard he tried, he could not convince his daughter of the truth of his statement. Finally, he said, "Hillary, why won't you believe me?" "Well," she said quite imperiously, "if the superintendent had five bosses, it would be bossy, bossy, bossy, bossy, bossy—and she would be all confused!"

I've shared this story with my board, and a number of other school boards, and the degree of laughter among these board members attests to the veracity of Hillary's observation. The story has served as a shorthand way to get the board back on track. In a meeting, for example, when board members were giving me conflicting directions, one board member looked at the other members and said, "bossy, bossy." The board members laughed and refocused to develop a single direction.

It doesn't always work, of course. However, the story is a good way to make a point and to remind people of the importance of clear direction.

The Complexity of Multiple Bosses

"While I felt confident about most aspects of the superintendency, I was completely unprepared for the complexity of working with five school board members."

In July of 1993 I accepted my first superintendency in a small rural town of 25,000 people. Growing up in small towns and raising my children in the Midwest, I was excited about working in a district of 4,600 students. It was an opportunity to learn every aspect of this exciting and challenging new role. After serving nearly 14 years in various administrative positions in Illinois and California, I thought I was well prepared with a broad array of knowledge, skills, and experiences to take on this new assignment.

It didn't take me long to realize that while I felt confident about most aspects of the superintendency, I was completely unprepared for the complexity of working with five school board members.

These five people all had relatives (children, mothers, spouses, cousins, siblings) who worked in some capacity for the district, and all of them had children in various schools in the district. There were many opportunities for serious conflicts of interest. One board member was married to the president of the support staff labor union; another was married to a high school counselor who was a member of the teachers' bargaining union. All had lived in the community for many years with collective memories about how the district had been managed in the past.

In order to have effective communication, I told the board members I would meet with each of them individually each month so we could talk about their issues one on one. I also said I hoped if there were concerns, they would contact me prior to our meetings so I could address them in a timely manner. I assured them I would call them individually whenever an important issue or event occurred.

I soon realized each member of the board had very specific ideas and issues of importance to them and their relatives. It was a delicate balancing act to listen carefully and to uncover and understand problems when this involved personal gain issues. Usually they seemed unaware their conversations included some aspect of their relatives' employment. Until I began to ask questions within the organization, I often didn't understand either. At one point it seemed everyone employed in the district was related to everyone else, but there had never been any district guidelines regarding nepotism, and clearly, no one wanted any.

I agreed to bring a report to the board after my first four months on the job with a preliminary analysis of district needs and the draft of a plan to meet those needs. This report was well received, and I was excited about setting out on a journey to lead and support the improvement of teaching and learning in our district.

My employment contract included a provision that the board would meet with me each year at the mid-point to conduct an informal review of my performance. In February we met on a Saturday morning to hold a Board Advance (we no longer retreat) in a conference room at City Hall. We discussed changes to the board agenda, the content of the reports in the board packet, the board handbook, and a variety of other details about how the board did its work.

I then asked the board to discuss my performance with me and make suggestions regarding ways I might improve. After their discussion, I gave them my perspective of how they were helping me and also what was hindering my efforts. I said that while the comments they passed on to me from their various relatives were informative, it was important we all stay focused on what we had agreed would be our mission.

I also said that the goals we were undertaking would take at least five years for us to see significant results. Determining content and performance standards, enhancing instructional strategies, and building a multiple measure achievement system would not happen overnight. There would be constant interruptions which would take time and use resources to address. However, we could not lose sight of what we were striving to achieve. They needed to work together to enable me and staff members to do our respective jobs.

When I reflected back on that meeting recently with the current board president, he laughed aloud and said it was a fond memory for him. He said he told his colleagues at the community college that he had never had a superintendent evaluate the board and give them directions for future actions.

I continue to deliver the same message to the board year after year, along with spending significant time with each member discussing their ideas and concerns. At the end of each conversation, I remind them what we must focus on and how important their support is in accomplishing the goals of the district. I also continue to struggle with such employee-employer relations as nepotism and employee favoritism among board members.

Boards Who Love You Can Be Difficult

"I soon learned that this dream board required as much time, caring and thought as previous, less harmonious boards."

You must be as careful and thoughtful with a board that loves you as one with whom you struggle. Anyone who's had only a difficult board may find that ludicrous, but it is true.

Moving from working with a troubled, contentious board to one thrilled to have me seemed unreal. I believed life would be simpler, the time with board members less and, therefore, time with students and staff much greater. After all, the new board members went to the annual school board's dinner wearing signs with sayings like "she won't need a bridge, she walks on water," and "eat your hearts out, look who we have." Wow! It doesn't get better than this.

I soon learned, however, that this dream board required as much time, caring and thought as previous, less harmonious boards. That is, if I wanted them to keep loving me. And I did!

Quickly it was apparent each board member noticed the amount of time and attention the other members had with me. Once I was appointed, my talented assistant clued me in when she set up initial meetings with each member.

I asked her to schedule breakfast or lunch meetings, thinking that having my first session with each member in a more casual setting would be the best way to start. After calls to three of the board members, she came into me with a smile on her face.

"You're quite a draw," she said. "They are trying to outdo each other. After I scheduled the first board member, the next two wanted to know where the others were taking you. Each call resulted in a fancier restaurant. By the fifth board member you'll be going to the top gourmet restaurant in the county!"

That situation was a piece of good luck. What I already knew about the importance of being fair and "the same" with each board member was reinforced—graphically.

Another opportunity to relearn this vital message appeared at the next board election when a person I had known for a long time was elected. This person was universally admired throughout the community and by the other board members. I figured this was truly board-superintendent heaven. Wrong!

Just when I thought I had figured out how to deal with jealousy within a board that loved me, it bubbled out in a new way. The new member, though loved by all, was now a threat to the fine balance we had achieved. It is very hard to pull back from relationships you enjoy, but "evenness with all" is a primary rule for superintendents and is essential for maintaining the professionalism and open communication necessary for a harmonious board.

The rule of evenness for all is important to teach those whom we mentor. I had a teachable moment with one of my deputy superintendents when he was a finalist for his first superintendency. As often happens, the board was coming to the district on a confirmation visit to talk with district staff and me. The board was all women, and four of the five came on the visit. About three minutes into my time with the board members, an alert flag went up. My early feelings about potential danger for my deputy rose throughout the meeting.

At the end of the board's visit, I told my deputy I had some insights to share with him. I told him about the rule of "evenness for all" and suggested he follow it very, very carefully! "Why?" "You haven't started yet and already they are all jealous of each other." He was puzzled. I reminded him he was a smart, energetic and handsome man and he had a board of five women. Yes, he and each board member were interested in the best education possible but he was naïve about the power of human feelings and emotions and the importance of managing them thoughtfully and carefully.

I offered a variety of strategies to minimize potential land mines for him, including: do not take one to lunch without taking each of them to lunch or breakfast or whatever, do not go anywhere in the evening with one alone, never say anything which one could interpret even slightly as anything other than professional interest, and take your wife with you to every event she's willing to attend.

The rule of "evenness with all" was the proper, ethical and professional practice I followed with a contentious board. I learned it was equally important in working with a harmonious board who hired me unanimously. So did my deputy.

BUILDING THE BOARD TEAM

"My belief that only people with good intentions run for the board was challenged."

People run for a board of education for a variety of reasons. They also come to the board role with diverse talents and sometimes with limited abilities and perspectives. An important responsibility of the superintendent is to provide training for board members, enabling them to be as effective as possible. The dilemma, however, is that boards change so training needs to be on-going. Good superintendents know that board training begins prior to the election.

Assumptions: Don't Make Them

"My fledgling assumptions as a superintendent were overturned and a new reality set in."

As a new superintendent, I immediately began creating a team focused on outstanding educational programs for all students. I assumed I had several months to pull everyone together, yet a short time into my tenure, I faced a board election. Fortunately, an experienced superintendent told me that the job of the superintendent in working with a board starts with candidate training before the election.

Following this advice, I developed information sessions for candidates, as well as for current board members who were running for re-election. These sessions not only informed the potential board members about the district, they also informed me about who might become a new board member "boss."

Facing an election is anxiety-producing, and often the anxiety increases after the election when new board members are elected. Assumptions about stability and support disappear, and they are replaced by harsh reality, a sense of insecurity and nagging thoughts about longevity. Of course, as a new superintendent, questions about longevity were never too far from my mind anyway.

As I became somewhat familiar with the candidates, my fledgling assumptions as a superintendent were overturned and a new reality set in. First, my assumption of a stable board vanished. Second, my belief that only people with good intentions run for the school board was challenged. I learned first-hand that voters don't take the time to sort out those candidates who care about children from those with personal or political agendas. I had to confront the reality that fairness and logic would not necessarily prevail. Finally, I came face to face with the possibility that things might not turn out for the best.

The reality of board elections is this: the chemistry of the board can change, literally, overnight. The change of even one board member takes us back to zero. No new group becomes a team automatically. It takes hard work, and the superintendent is the only one who can make it happen. If the superintendent doesn't do it, it does not happen.

After the election I was responsible for pulling five unique people together to work for all the children in the district. I knew that present board members would help pull the board together, but it was my job. With every member of the board, I had to think about ways to bring that person into the team. I listened, talked, listened, talked, and listened some more.

Central to developing the team, I had to learn and understand why each board member wanted to be on the board. What goals, desires and dreams did each one have? I could not satisfy their needs and help them fulfill their desires as board members without knowing their individual goals. Yet despite their individual goals, I had a responsibility to make them see the big picture and become effective in realizing the larger issues facing the district.

Most school administrators spend their careers with one direct boss. Few of us are prepared to have multiple bosses. The outcome of working with and for five people with individual ideas of what a district needs, and what you as superintendent should do, coupled with all the other aspects of this challenging new role, is a whole rethinking of all your assumptions!

Tips on Handling Board Elections

As superintendent I face the inescapable fact that school board elections occur every two years, and depending on the cycle, there are two or three seats up for election each time. This means there are internal and external processes to monitor.

The Internal Process

Experience has taught me that the superintendent must be certain guidelines are developed and distributed so site administrators know how to handle inappropriate campaign activities by board candidates. It can be challenging for site administrators and superintendents to deal with board candidates who do not want to follow the rules and who push the limits of acceptable practice. When confronted with this situation, a site administrator needs to make immediate contact with the superintendent. Guidelines should have a legal foundation and practical suggestions to deal with issues in a commonsense manner. Site administrators then should be held accountable for knowing and following the guidelines.

The External Process

The person in charge of public relations must be aware of campaign laws, communication protocols, and material distribution. It is important that the information officer or designated communicator from the district be in a position to provide wise counsel to organizations and community members, as well as those at the school site. For example, while PTAs do not generally endorse candidates, they usually have forums where candidates are allowed to express their views. Close communication with school district information staff and PTA organizations can enhance communication.

Do's and Don'ts

During my thirteen years as a superintendent, I have learned the following lessons about board elections:

1. Be sure all administrators are aware of the legal and political ramifications of taking a position on board candidates.
2. The public information officer, or appropriate staff member, should send a bulletin advising all administrators what they can and cannot do.
3. Use discretion when dealing with the press. The press will try to elicit your opinions or preferences about candidates. Avoid this above all.
4. Stay out of the politics as much as possible. Consider whether or not to attend forums, and never give opinions which could be interpreted as supportive of a particular candidate.
5. Be prepared to conduct a candidate's briefing prior to the election to give candidates information about the school district.
6. When the election process is over, send a congratulatory letter to the successful candidate(s). Also send letters to the unsuccessful candidates thanking them for their interest in the school system.

After elections, I recognize the need to work with all board members, newly elected and continuing. The best advice I follow is to treat all board members alike even though new board members need extra time for training and information. In working with the new members, I do not treat them as uninformed, but rather as people who need more information and who are eager for assistance. With regard to continuing board members, I make certain I continue to provide the atmosphere that demonstrates the board operates as a whole unit, not as an advocate for special interest groups.

The best advice for a superintendent is to keep an objective view of all aspects of a board election. There is a natural tendency for community and staff to persuade the superintendent to take an active role in board, city and other elections. Above all, *avoid* this. Such behavior can lead to professional suicide.

Revolving Board Members

"A very stable board who had worked together for a while faced an amazing number of changes. In fact, over the next eleven months, we had ten new members with only one original board member still on the board."

As every superintendent knows, the composition of the board changes on a regular basis. At the very least, two members are up for election every two years. Some are re-elected, some are not, and some decide not to run again. After an election, the remaining board members and the superintendent must work with the new board members to assist them in how to be a board member and to provide them with information about the district. As long as the new board members do not have personal agendas different from those of the existing board members, this process works very well.

For six years that was how we worked. After each election, the remaining board and I would spend time with the one or two new board members. This process allowed for a smooth transition for the existing board and for the new board members.

In one year, this all changed. A very stable board who had worked together for a while faced an amazing number of changes. In fact, over the next eleven months, we had ten new members with only one original board member still on the board.

No one could have predicted these changes which started in October. One board member was transferred to another state; another chose not to run in November, leaving his seat open; and still another board member ran and did not get re-elected. One board member ran for a four-year seat even though he still had two years left on his term and was elected, which left his two-year seat vacant. A new board member was elected in November. With the election of an existing board member and the transfer of the other, two seats were still open that needed to be filled by appointment. Two board members were appointed in December, giving us a full board until February, when one of the original board members resigned for family reasons. In March that seat was filled by appointment. In August, one of the Board members appointed in December resigned because he moved out of the district's boundaries, which created the tenth change.

With four of the five board members new, we had to change how we operated. Every board meeting became a training session, starting with such basics as how to make a motion. Instead of meeting in small groups, we needed to meet frequently in day-long meetings to provide information on what was happening in the district.

Fortunately, we had individuals who cared deeply about being good board members. They agreed to attend as many California School Boards Association (CSBA) programs as they could to learn about their new role. We had CSBA leaders guide a one-day session on how board members should work with each other and with the superintendent.

The extra time we spent was well worth it. The new board members worked hard to develop good skills. Because of the extra work they did, after only four months they were able to function as though they had worked together for years.

Orientation and Ongoing Training

"After the most recent election in my district, I learned the two new board members who defeated the incumbents did not want to spend any time touring the district with me. They both told me they believed they already knew everything they needed to know and were not interested in hearing anything from my perspective."

The major challenge of the superintendency is working successfully with the board. Since the composition of boards typically changes at least every two years, the superintendent must assume the responsibility for orientation of new board members and the ongoing training of experienced board members.

Even before the board election, most superintendents conduct an orientation session for those who have filed as candidates. Orientation sessions typically cover a broad overview of all aspects of the district and specifics on district goals and priorities, followed by questions and answers. Unfortunately, sometimes candidates do not attend any board meetings and therefore are not only unaware of the general operation of the school district, but they are also unaware of critical challenges and issues unique to the district.

I invite all candidates, including the incumbents, to the orientation. I also invite our local representative on the county board of trustees as well as the three assistant superintendents for business, learning, and human resources. We spend approximately one-and-one-half hours on the role of the board, policies, plans, and budgets, and we provide copies of the annual reports of each division. We conclude the meeting by answering questions and offering to provide additional information and documents which will help them have a strong foundation of information about the district. We assure them that subsequent to all meetings, should one person request information, it will be sent to all candidates, ensuring equal access to the same information for everyone.

After the election, we invite newly elected board members to participate in a more in-depth orientation session prior to their formal seating on the board. I offer to take them on a tour of the district and to give them a briefing of issues and concerns from my perspective.

Twice each year, I held a Board Advance for about five hours on a Saturday morning. We have met in a large conference room at City Hall and brought in snacks and sandwiches for lunch. The agendas typically included review, revision, and discussion of all aspects of board meetings from the seating arrangement to how information is presented. We have contracted with consultants to help us improve our communication skills, learn about the budget, and study facilities needs and consider how to finance those needs. These meetings are more informal than regular board meetings, and board members have consistently reported that these sessions are of great value.

No Surprises

> "A wise person once advised me that a good superintendent never lets her board feel unprepared or unsupported in public."

"Believe in Yourself" is a song from *The Wiz*, a musical stage and screen adaptation of Frank Baum's *The Wonderful Wizard of Oz*. The lyrics of this song tell the travelers to Oz that if they believe in themselves, they will have the brains, the heart and the courage they desire to "last their whole life through."

As a superintendent, I have discovered that if I sustain a strong belief in myself and my team, we can accomplish just about anything in record time. Admittedly, there will be long days and a few sleepless nights, but the exhilaration of accomplishment cannot be underestimated. After a recent election, California superintendents and boards were faced with a serious challenge because of the passage of yet another proposition designed to reform public education. We had sixty days to design, secure board approval and begin a program for English-language learners that virtually changed the way in which we provided their instruction for the past twenty-five years.

I met with the Education Services staff and we developed a plan. I developed a board report on the implications of this new law for our schools and outlined the board's responsibility. During that meeting, the staff listened politely to the barrage of questions and comments. We also assured our board that our program would meet the letter and the spirit of the law. This was very important to at least three members of the board who were facing a fall election campaign. For this important special meeting, I prepared a color slide presentation and made sure that the board and news media had printed copies of my slides. My goal was to make certain that when questions arose about this new law, the board was not caught off guard. A wise person once advised me that a good superintendent never lets her board feel unprepared or unsupported in public.

Since this new law was vehemently opposed by our bilingual staff, but embraced by two thirds of the voting public, we reasoned that implementing the new law would require that our board and administrative staff display the intellect (brains), the empathy (heart) and the boldness (courage) sought by the travelers to Oz. The test of the acceptance of this program and support for our belief that we must be meticulous in the design phase of any project requiring rapid system-wide change came when school opened in the fall. We received not a single request from parents to offer a bilingual program. This situation remained throughout the first quarter of the school year. One of our board members expressed an opinion that parents did not really understand their rights. In response to his concerns, and to ensure that parents received information in a format that met their needs, we developed an extensive outreach strategy. Our approach included bilingual brochures describing program options and outlining parents' rights, a question and answer document for parents, announcements for play on Spanish-language radio stations, district-wide and school-site bilingual parent meetings, and notices in Spanish-language newspapers.

Knowing that teachers ultimately determine the success of any important change, our Language Services staff developed a question and answer document for teachers, outlined specific requirements of instruction in the three program models specified in the law, and sought teachers' opinions about the best ESOL materials available. Within two weeks these materials arrived in the district and were delivered to sites. The coordinator made site visits to every school to answer questions about issues that confronted teachers during the first few weeks of school and reported favorably on the instruction students were receiving.

As a superintendent, I knew that it was my responsibility to ensure that the voting public and the conservative factions in the district recognized we were implementing the new law. So that board members would not be surprised by questions from the public, I made two presentations to two committees of the local Chamber of Commerce. At one meeting, my belief in our insistence on meticulous planning and faithful implementation was reinforced when, after answering a few questions about how we were implementing this new law, the publisher of one of our weekly newspapers was very complimentary about the quality of our plan for educating English learners. After he spoke, two other influential members of the community spoke up and said, "The school district always does a good job in implementing new programs; look what they did with class size reduction." For that moment, I had reached Oz.

THE WAVY LINE BETWEEN POLICY AND ADMINISTRATION

"With the diversity of motives people possess who choose to be board members . . . the issue of who's running the district will continue to be a challenge for a superintendent."

Boards of education, and all their employees, have roles, legal requirements, and important responsibilities. Policy is the true and primary task for boards, and this policy provides direction to everyone in the organization. How boards carry out their roles, and how the superintendent guides them, is critical to the school district's success.

What constitutes policy setting and administration? This is often one of the most challenging and controversial aspects of dealing with the board. When the lines blur between the two, the term frequently heard is "micromanagement of the superintendent."

Revisiting the Board's Purpose

"Micromanagement most commonly occurs when board members ask themselves questions such as "What purpose do I serve as a governing board member? When do I have a say in a matter that may not be a policy?"

Superintendents find walking the line between policy and administration is a problematic aspect of the job. It is particularly troubling when
one or more board members assume the responsibility for a job that is
clearly the superintendent's or that of another district administrator.

The challenge is in how micromanagement is defined and dealt with.
I have handled this by keeping a chronology, or a log, when issues or
activities arise which fall under my heading of micromanagement. This
allows me to see trends of micromanagement over time, and when appropriate, call it to the board members' attention.

A graphic example of such a situation occurred when I received a
phone call from a board member who requested an appointment. During the meeting the board member informed me that one of our community members had just been diagnosed with a serious health problem. This parent had a long professional relationship with the board
member. Because of this long-time relationship, any time a school issue
occurred, the parent felt that the proper way of dealing with it was to
call the board member—not the teacher, not the principal, nor anyone
else who may have been involved. Therefore, a pattern of improper
communication was established that became comfortable and, unfortunately, normal.

The board member indicated she was going to have to become an advocate for this parent due to these challenging health issues. This ad-
vocacy related to a request for a track change for the child of the parent. Complicating matters was the fact that the parent/family had not
met clearly established criteria for being considered for a track change.
I listened for a long time as the board member presented her case.
When she finished, I asked one question: "Are you directing me to automatically, over normal process or criteria, make a track change for
this child at your direction? You know it would violate the criteria, and
even if it did, it would move this parent to the head of the list because
of your preferential treatment?" The board member replied that this
was not her intent at all.

When I put the issue in context and raised my concern regarding
proper board behavior, the board member saw my viewpoint and the
larger consequences and withdrew her request. Ultimately there was
space for the child in the track and the request was granted. However,
the board member redirected the parent back to the original process.
Important lessons were learned by the board member as well as the
parent.

Micromanagement most commonly occurs when board members ask themselves questions such as "What purpose do I serve as a governing board member? When do I have a say in a matter that may not be a policy?" My experience is that board members who are clear about policy versus administration, who have no ulterior motive, who have no axes to grind, and who truly want a superintendent to lead, sort this out well. My experience is also that board members who want to be administrators, want to control, and do not understand or care about the difference between policy and administration will always have a problem with this.

The role of the superintendent in all of these cases is to maintain a definition of policy versus administration, and most importantly, to use persuasion, examples, and clear communication to help board members see the difference. It is important to have a clear policy on which everyone can rely. The policy should clarify that a board member is only a board member when acting as a member of a governing board, and a board member has no authority to direct the work of any employee or commit the district to any expenditure of money.

With the diversity of motives people possess who choose to be board members, coupled with increased union attempts to control board members, the issue of who's running the district will continue to be a challenge for a superintendent.

Honoring Board Policy

"My final approach was to pointedly ask this board member if he wanted me to violate the board's policy."

Hiring a competent superintendent is the most important job of the board. The second is policymaking. Ironically, I have found that adhering to policy is a most difficult task for some board members.

My conflict with board member adherence to policy began with a board member who made a habit of criticizing one particular principal. On several occasions during closed sessions or telephone calls, he indicated concern about the principal. In his opinion, she had not been able to control criticism of certain teachers by an outside militant activist group identified by newspaper reports as disruptive to the operation of several school districts. His contention was that teachers felt unsupported. Nothing I could say seemed to convince him that the principal was doing an admirable job and, with assistance from district staff, was working effectively toward solutions.

This board member asked me to accompany him on visits to several of our school campuses. It was the first time in four years we visited campuses together. He asked that we include in our visits the campus which was the focus of his criticism.

As we toured the campus, the principal did everything to elicit a favorable response about something on the campus, but nothing seemed to please the board member. This campus was one of the cleanest and most orderly in the district. The principal had initiated numerous grant proposals to ensure that all children were reading. She also worked as director of a summer staff development institute for teachers.

During an assembly program, I noticed the board member walking up to several teachers, engaging them in conversation. As we drove to another campus, this board member continued to ask how the principal was working to control the activists. He said he heard complaints from teachers that she had hired the critics as playground supervisors. I responded that if the teachers had a complaint, they should follow our board policy.

Several months later one of the teachers called my office asking, on behalf of a group, for an appointment to discuss their concerns about the principal, The teacher indicated they had met with the assistant superintendent, but were dissatisfied with the response. She followed this request with a letter containing undocumented claims against the principal. After receiving my letter of response, this teacher forwarded her complaint with my response to this board member. In a surprise move during closed session, the board member questioned me about the complaint and harshly asked me why I had not informed the board of this problem, since they were to know everything that was going on in the district.

My typical demeanor with board members is usually low key and my responses are measured. This time I felt my response was related directly to board policy. I indicated that according to policy, it was my job to administer the district and at this point, the matter had not properly reached the board level. I also noted, according to the board's own policy, this teacher and her colleagues had skipped several steps in taking their case directly to a board member. The teachers had not demonstrated any reasonable effort to confer with the principal. Further, they made references to unsubstantiated potential retaliation as the reason for not meeting with their principal to work out a solution as required in our policy.

My final approach was to pointedly ask this board member if he wanted me to violate the board's policy. The other board members sat by silently as I traded words with their colleague who became more and more strident and unreasonable. I finally tried a strategy I would consider a once in a lifetime tactic: I polled the board. The other board members said I should continue on my present course and if and when the subject reached their level, they would deal with it.

Since that time, it is very easy for me, when board members make a request outside of the boardroom or ask me to follow up on a matter clearly requiring board approval, to remind them that the entire board is responsible for making certain decisions.

Board members frequently begin their requests with the phrase, "I am not trying to micromanage, but. . . ." I believe they really are asking if they are in line with our policies and the laws concerning the conduct of members of public boards. I often remind them it is my job to keep them out of trouble, and we have a good laugh.

Shaping Up Board Policies

"In today's world, being without current board policies is akin to tightrope walking without a net."

It is not unusual to start your superintendency and find outdated board policies—or none at all. In my new district, I was first relieved to be without a *War and Peace*–size book of rules, but the reality was that in today's world, being without current board policies is akin to tightrope walking without a net.

Shaping up board policies is an onerous, even Herculean, task. Yet it is a job a superintendent can use to move a district forward to a higher level of professionalism. The fact was, in my new district, the policies I could find were last updated twenty years earlier. The majority of existing policies had little or no value and were often contradictory with current law.

My approach was to review district guidelines in other forms, such as school handbooks and personnel documents, before sharing with the board the current status of district policies. In my weekly written communications with the board, I told the board about my analysis of what we had in place and that I was working to find the gaps that together (board and superintendent) we would fill.

Before I talked about specific needs, I worked with the board on our philosophy regarding policies. I suggested we view this process as an important way to develop a working relationship around critical processes. The policies were "their work" and how to carry out the policies was "my work," but we would be a team.

Our state had a board policy development service that we used as a guide. The board agreed we did not need policies that were already covered by the state education code, the government code or other law. Therefore, we could focus on policies directly affecting our district. This enabled us to have discussions that were related to our district's philosophy.

Another successful approach was adopting many policies or whole sections at once, rather than one at a time. This mega-approach gave the board the big picture and minimized having each policy nit-picked to death.

At the time of adoption, when board members had questions staff or I could not answer, or when a board member suggested a direction I was unsure about, I requested more time to study the issue. I did not want to rush to adoption and have to fix a policy later.

Once the initial policies were in place, we set a regular time, at least once a year, to update the policies. Each year new laws are passed, so new policies and revisions are always necessary, but a regular review of existing policies is also essential. The updating of policies is time consuming, but inadequate or out-of-date, and sometimes illegal, policies put your district at risk.

BOARD MEETINGS: GETTING DOWN TO REAL BUSINESS

"As the lesson plan guides the classroom teacher, the board meeting agenda is the centerpiece of effective board meetings. The agenda is the work product of the superintendent."

Board meetings are the public presentation of the district's business. Preparation for them is critical to how the board and the superintendent are viewed by the community. The board agenda is the superintendent's work product and sends a message about priorities while the conduct of the meeting demonstrates the working relationship, the teamwork, among the board members and the superintendent.

Surprises can occur at meetings, and superintendents need to anticipate what might occur. Experience tells us that these meetings can be exhilarating and exhausting. As a result, superintendents need to think about what to do following the meeting to ensure they move forward in a positive way.

Planning the Meeting

"During those early months, I wasn't sure how to construct an agenda, nor did I ever think that it could be a creative, interesting, and innovative document."

I often recall my first months as a new superintendent. I had attended dozens of board meetings as a school site and district administrator, and had dutifully followed the board agenda from beginning to end. The formats always seemed a little confusing and the language filled with jargon that only the educators in the audience seemed to understand. Few people attended the board meetings. I understood why. The meetings were rather dull and lifeless. The only times the meetings were enthusiastic were when students were honored for their academic, sports, or fine arts performances. But most of the time it was business as usual.

During those early months, I wasn't sure how to construct an agenda, nor did I ever think that it could be a creative, interesting, and innovative document. I found out soon that I wasn't alone in my reflection on how boring board agendas and board meetings could be.

And yet, board meetings are the most significant event in the superintendent's and boards' monthly calendar. As the lesson plan guides the classroom teacher, the board meeting agenda is the centerpiece of effective board meetings. The agenda is the work product of the superintendent. It is the highly visible documentation of the work of the administrative team.

A few years into the superintendency, I jumped at the opportunity to chair the new superintendent's portion of the annual conference, which is attended by nearly 900 superintendents in the state. During an informal sampling of experienced superintendents, I found that construction of an effective agenda which reflected effective organizational management was high on the need list. They said they really needed this support as new superintendents and would be very interested in how colleagues approach this important task.

I gathered agendas from small-, medium- and large-sized elementary, high school, and unified districts. Some were stapled, others were coil bound and in binders. They were color coded, tabbed, highlighted with district logos, or simply plain vanilla covers. The array was remarkable.

We developed a thick document with samples of shortened versions and detailed agendas, postmeeting highlights and news releases about upcoming events. And the success of this document was legendary the first year! Not only were new superintendents clamoring for this set of agendas from districts throughout the state, but also experienced school leaders were gathered around them as a source of a fresh look for their important district work. Dozens of ideas emerged in these materials which have positively assisted colleagues throughout the state.

Highlights and "best practices" in agenda setting and board documentation include:

The District's Vision and Mission

The district's mission and vision statements are often boldly printed on agendas to remind participants that all district tasks should reflect district goals. Often, the district's core values highlight operational beliefs. Accompanying the broader statements are focus areas or core values to which the district is committed. Examples are participatory leadership, parent involvement, or interest-based decision making.

Special Presentations to the Board

At the beginning of most board agendas, there is special time set aside to involve and acknowledge stakeholders of the organization. By establishing a standard time for these important presentations, boards acknowledge the importance of wide involvement in the district by staff, parents, and community members. Presentations could be by student board members, student leadership organizations, parents, chambers of commerce, local service clubs, school sites, curriculum teams, grade-level leaders, faculty groups, mentor teachers. There are many possibilities.

Special Acknowledgments by the Board

Boards often set aside important times for public acknowledgment of the contributions made by such organizational groups. Not coincidentally, school districts with strong track records of student performance are districts in which board agendas reflect ongoing participation and acknowledgment of the collaboration between contributing organizations. Examples of special presentations by board members are those made to retirees, long-term employees, leaders of food drives, championship athletic and academic teams, mock trial teams and essay contest winners. Others are athletic booster organizations, business partners, county offices of education, coordinating councils, and religious organizations. An expansive array of board presentations to a wide range of participants symbolically reflects a board's commitment to acknowledge and welcome wide involvement in the important work of the district.

Agenda Format

Agenda documents are often tabbed, color coded by department or differentiated by the use of traditional papers or card stock. The agendas are ring bound, presented in binders, power stapled, or clipped together and placed in file folders. Within the document, detailed information often includes names of board members and district personnel, board meeting calendar dates and highlights of frequently-used organization tips like those outlined in *Robert's Rules of Order*.

The design of the agenda includes items related to each organizational entity within the district. Information, discussion and action items are generally presented under the heading of superintendent, business services, education services and personnel. The order of presentation and the level of detail provided to the board varies based on priorities or is set and followed at each meeting. The items often include organizational steps such as background, description, and fiscal impact, funding source, and staff recommendations regarding the item. The level of information provided reflects the item's importance, complexity, or the detail requested by the individual board. Closed-session agendas list items for confidential discussion and strictly follow legal requirements. These sessions on confidential matters are most often held before the regular board meeting with continuations held after meetings as necessary.

Community Involvement

In every board agenda, there is a portion for participation by the public. Often referred to as the public comment section of the agenda, this is often at the beginning of the meeting to allow maximum participation. Agendas frequently include guidelines and legal requirements for public participation and board and/or staff response. Some boards schedule a social period at the beginning or at a transition point after presentations to allow community members to visit informally with board members on a range of interests while having refreshments. Ranging from fifteen to forty-five minutes, this informal interchange allows relationships to build and provides accessibility to board members and staff on a regularly scheduled basis.

Meeting Times and Lengths

From Monday through Thursday, board meetings are started from early afternoon to 8 p.m. at the latest with most starting between 6:30 and 7:30 p.m. Meetings last from one to several hours. To control meeting length, a trend is emerging to print time limits for each item on the agenda to facilitate meeting flow. Some boards have guidelines for meeting length to which all members agree. For example, if a 7 p.m. board meeting is anticipated to last beyond the stated 9:30 p.m. limit, at 9:00 p.m., the board must agree to extend the meeting to 10 p.m. by mutual consent. Special meetings on topical interests are often scheduled during evenings and weekends to allow longer periods of time for research, study and reflection.

Communications with Colleagues

Superintendents invariably learn new tips or strategies to effectively facilitate the board meetings by consulting colleagues on the range of approaches to developing effective board agendas. Sharing documents, approaches, formats, placement of items, details and effective timelines for accomplishing the business of the district is essential. As a public relations tool, nothing is as significant as having a board agenda document that is easily understood and rich in detail.

Concluding Comments

The board agenda is the most important ongoing document shared with the greater community. Significant efforts must be made by the superintendent to present a document which reflects the district's mission, organization, and effectiveness. A well-presented document, which facilitates efficient and effective meetings, will elicit the confidence of a wide range of participants in the school district. Most importantly, it will provide the necessary foundation information for the board to make confident and well-grounded decisions on behalf of the students of the district.

Board Meeting Twists Keep You on Your Toes

"Foreshadowing the change was the appearance of the husband of the new majority leader who came into the meeting room with his video camcorder."

"The Board Meeting that Started It All" was how we began to refer to the beginning of a major change in how board meetings occurred in our district. We approached the reorganization meeting following a board election with some anxiety. A new majority would be in power, one with an ultraconservative philosophy. Clearly, change was eminent. What no one anticipated was the enormity of the change, brought on by someone who had never attended a board meeting before. No amount of planning or no attention to detail could have prepared us, or prevented what happened. It is a perfect example of why most superintendents say they have a "pit" in their stomachs the day of board meetings.

Foreshadowing the change was the appearance of the husband of the new majority leader who came into the meeting room with his video camcorder. With his camera rolling, the meeting began with an air of tension and civility with the election of board officers, and the new majority elected each other to the various offices on 3–2 votes. Then came the usually innocuous "Public Comment" section of the meeting. A biologist from a nearby university stood up, addressed the board holding a fossil in his hand and demanded of the board, "I want to know your intentions about this. Do you intend to bury this evidence of the evolution of man and impose your beliefs on students of this district?" In response, a member of the board minority requested the item be placed for discussion on the next meeting's agenda.

That statement and response changed the course of the district for the next two years. Board meetings that normally drew the usual fifteen to twenty interested observers became media events overnight.

From around the country, media calls deluged our office the day following that first meeting of the new majority and the biologist's question. It was clear that meetings could no longer be held in the traditional boardroom with a capacity of seventy-five. Anticipating a large attendance, we scheduled the next meeting for a school's multipurpose room. However, that proved to be too small and meetings thereafter were held in a school gymnasium.

Planning for board meetings had always been an important event, but now it took on a high stakes feel. The agenda and backup continued to be the focus, but now we needed to pay attention to how to deal with the media. Topics included preparing press releases, designating a spokesperson on various issues and decisions regarding where to put the press table and how to create space for media equipment. It was a time of learning multiple lessons. I always knew that being "Out among the troops" as Donald Phillips writes in *Lincoln on Leadership*, was important, but during these tumultuous years, personal and written communication following board meetings was critical. I prepared Board Highlights that summarized the board meetings. In addition, all of the district leaders were prepared to state clearly the facts of board actions.

An unexpected outcome, and one of the few pleasant ones for me, was hearing from relatives I hadn't seen in many years calling to ask, "Was that you I saw on CNN?"

Recovering from the Meeting

Early in my career as a superintendent I learned about the importance of recovering from each board meeting. Everyone on the staff understands the importance of planning for the meeting—deciding which items go on the agenda, writing clear and concise information about each item, determining their placement, anticipating questions that each board member might ask and preparing for any community concern or comments. I believe that following up after each meeting is as important as preparing for one.

The day after the meeting I bring all of the cabinet members together to debrief the meeting. We go over our notes and decide who will follow up on any questions that arose during the meeting. We critique our presentations and consider how we might present future items more clearly. We consider what information we need to get out to board members before a future topic hits the agenda or what type of community work needs to be done to address controversial or difficult issues. We talk about the process and content of the meeting, and we find ways to laugh about relatively mundane topics.

After a meeting at which the teachers' union and classified union conducted an unusually loud and raucous demonstration about their lack of an acceptable salary increase and the singing of a well-known song with lyrics that challenged my leadership ability, the value of our debriefing meeting became especially clear to all of us. At the beginning of the meeting we glumly reviewed our own personal points of view about the demonstration. As we continued our debriefing one of the cabinet members quietly expressed her disappointment and jealousy that no one sang a song about her, and suddenly we all burst into laughter. For a few brief minutes we all found ways to relieve the carryover tension of this meeting by considering other songs that could be sung by us at a future meeting.

This kind of lighthearted interaction plays an important role in dealing with the stress and tension that frequently occurs at meetings of the board held in public. Ultimately, the camaraderie of our debriefings helps all of us to put the discussions and activities of board meetings into perspective and to get on with the important work of the organization. We know that public meetings are an integral part of our work as public educators and that public input is to be taken seriously. We also know, however, that we must stay focused on the mission and goals of the organization and not be discouraged or dismayed by negative or challenging comments. Recovering from meetings is an important aspect of our daily lives.

LESSONS LEARNED

We have learned a few lessons about working with board members, truths that keep the journey challenging and exciting.

- Remember it takes a majority vote to get direction.
- Treat all board members alike.
- Make sure you have a board evaluation process in place.
- Give the same information to every board member.
- Focus on board members' interests and goals.

- Understand that many factors affect your relationship with each board member.
- Work for consensus about what must be done, despite what individual board members want.
- Communicate, communicate, communicate.
- Make, and follow, a "no surprises" rule.
- Take periodic stock of the organization's progress.
- Understand that a change in one board member takes you back to zero—one new board member creates a new team.
- Recognize that not everyone is on the board for the sake of children.
- Have strategies for dealing with wild hares.
- Be a public servant, not a servant.
- Tell and show the board what you do.
- Get board policies in shape.
- Hold premeetings to ensure board members have adequate information to make decisions.
- Communicate actions after board meetings.
- Put board members out front.
- Have a mission, themes, and values—and keep them in the forefront at all times.
- Model what you want.
- Be proactive and make contact with each board member every week.
- Be visible and in touch to prevent "stuff" that could become problematic.
- Call each board member the day before you leave for vacation and the day you return.

Chapter 3

Knowing Your
Organization and Its People

"In our organizations, there are wonderful people, who, in order to
remain productive, contributing members of the management team,
need a supportive boost. . . . Sometimes the superintendent is the
only person who can provide that extra boost to move a person to the
next level of confidence."

Every organization has a structure. The structure is both formal and
informal. Typically, the formal structure is represented through an
organizational chart. Such an organizational chart must be clearly understood in order to communicate effectively with all individuals
within the system.

The structure of an organization, no matter how small or large, new
or long established, requires that to be effective, the superintendent understand all elements of the system. Making assumptions or decisions
without this clear and comprehensive understanding is a sure way to
contribute to the demise of the superintendent and possibly the organization itself.

A few of the most important aspects of an organization are: communication systems and procedures, informal and formal network-
ing, internal and external policies, access and accountability
"norms," priority-setting, evaluation systems, personnel practices, and
decision-making authority and policies.

FIGURING OUT WHAT'S GOING ON

Listen First

"You called us all a bunch of wimps."

A month after I had arrived in the new school district and after I had spent time conducting a lengthy assessment session with each individual principal, I convened my first informal brown bag lunch meeting with thirty-two principals. It was an interactive session with an open agenda. Towards the end of the meeting, someone raised his hand and asked, "What is your impression of the principals so far?" Off the top of my head, I responded, "you are the most passive group of administrators I have ever worked with." My immediate thought was oops, what an insulting statement. After moments of silence a brave soul asked, "What do you expect of us?" I stated, "I expect you to question and challenge the status quo. Is doing what we have always done making a difference for our children today?"

It was three weeks before I received a phone call from a member of the group informing me that he finally got my message. I asked him what that was and he shared, "You called us all a bunch of wimps."

Later I learned the cultural norm for the organization was no questions asked. The act of questioning was perceived as an act of disrespect and disloyalty. The organization had operated on a comfortable paternalistic model which provided prescriptions for implementation and protection from individual responsibility. Values of conformity, compliance, and no-conflict were held in high regard. Don't rock the boat and don't talk about problems were acceptable operational behaviors.

It seems ironic that we can all recite the attributes and skills our students need for success in the twenty-first century, such as higher-order thinking skills, team work, problem solving, living with ambiguity, etc., and yet we fail to ask who they are going to learn from if the adults around them do not have it.

I have learned to be conscientious in my daily work to provoke questioning, to create discomfort, disequilibrium, and ambiguity and to raise the level of anxiety. This is not as easy to accomplish as I had anticipated and the backlash can be hurtful. Principals who seek greater autonomy for school-based decisions do not always accept the responsibility and accountability for outcomes.

Individual administrators plead for defining new rules and the cry "tell us what to do and we will do it" is still a common phrase. The sense of frustration is genuine, and it is an on-going struggle to balance solution-giving and questioning-thinking responses.

It would certainly be more convenient to give the "right answer" and quick fixes rather than to generate an inquiry process to create meaningful alternatives for systemic change.

The analogy which evokes similar feelings is when I have an overwhelmingly long day and I come home to a child who needs help with her homework. It would be less time-consuming and less frustrating for both of us if I would simply give the answer to the problem. It is a tempting solution, but I have to remember who gains the benefit and the responsibility for thinking. How do we think without questioning? How do we expect students to gain what we do not give?

Shifting the Power Structure

> "I remember my start as a new superintendent—excitement, fear, and a recognition that I really did not know what to do. Can anyone really understand what this role requires or what the title means to others?"

My doctoral dissertation had examined the politics of the superintendency, and I had done a classic literature review that focused on power. Yet I failed to comprehend the power the role can have and the effect on the power structure of the district the superintendent has.

The four staff people who were destined to be closest to me in my new adventure were the two secretaries in my office and the two assistant superintendents. Their tenure in the district ranged from fifteen to thirty-four years. I was the new kid on the block. I also followed a superintendent who had spent over ten years in the job.

Little did I see, at first, how my title conveyed power or how I could, and did, change who was perceived to have power.

I recall asking a question about the location of a table or file cabinet in one area of the office. The next day it had been rearranged, changed to fit what I had asked. It was meant as a question, but it had become a command to someone. Being sensitive to others, I began to realize that what I said, no matter how trivial it was to me, was going to carry weight.

Nothing quite prepared me for the power plays that would go on as I defined my role in the district. Both assistant superintendents had been long-time acquaintances and were very excited that I was selected for the job. Both secretaries, on the other hand, seemed less than thrilled. They were very loyal to the previous superintendent and were, it appeared to me, very reluctant to make a change.

When I interviewed each individual in the district office and talked with principals, it was evident that the two secretaries were viewed as very powerful and some level of resentment existed over that power. I'm not sure they even understood the power they held. They handled ordering of supplies for others in the office, student attendance accounting, all conferences, and technology in addition to the typical superintendent's secretarial responsibilities.

My initial assessment suggested, as did the two assistant superintendents, that some of these tasks really belonged in other offices. I began to make some changes. That's when things became interesting in terms of who was seen as powerful.

While some were pleased to see the control slip from my office staff, it added some power to the assistant superintendents. Both these men had felt somewhat diminished in power prior to my arrival, but, with the changes I was making, they gained some, at least in their eyes. But could they handle it effectively? Would they mishandle this newfound power? Would my secretaries be able to handle the loss of control? Would I survive the interplay of these struggles as I defined my style as superintendent?

I cleared my office of responsibilities that belonged elsewhere and opened it up for my priorities. This change didn't completely turn out the way I had planned. The secretaries were somewhat resentful, even though their workload was reduced. Others in the office, however, appreciated that their input had been valued. The changes helped to shift the power structure from an old paradigm to a new one. I know I made some mistakes in those early days. However, I learned a great deal about how power affects the structure of the organization. I also learned how critical it was to pay attention to how power plays out in the operation of a school system.

Getting Your Priorities Straight: The Importance of Showing Up

> "'Little Things Mean a Lot' was a popular song in the 1970s. Little does one know how significant 'little things' are."

One day in 1977, when I was a first-year bilingual teacher in a large suburban school district in Illinois, I remember how strongly I wished that the Principal or the Director of Bilingual Education or just anyone else had shown up to see the incredible performance of my class. These students, all of whom were learning English as a second language, had just performed an English rendition of "Chicken Little." Of course, the dialogue was not exactly like the script. There had been some improvisation along with a few hesitations and prompts from the rest of the class, who served as the audience. Overall, in my opinion, the performance was worthy of an Emmy nomination! Olga Martinez, a first grader from a rural area in Mexico, who had started the school year with just two words in English, gave the award-winning performance of her short acting career. Sadly, I thought, the other twenty-four students and I were the only ones who knew it.

Throughout that school year, neither the principal nor anyone from the district office came to visit our classroom. We sent out lots of handwritten or mimeographed invitations for special events, and many parents were able to find the time in their busy lives to come and witness the amazing performances of these students, but our classroom didn't make it onto the calendars of administrators. When I told my fellow teachers about how disappointed I was that no one showed up, they chided me for being so naïve as to assume that the principal or anyone else would have time to visit my classroom. I responded with outrage that they were accepting the fact that those who should be the best informed about what was happening in the classroom would not have first-hand knowledge about actual practice.

In 1988, I left that district and came to California to work in a large suburban district at the central office level. By that time, I was convinced that "showing up" was a very important part of an administrator's job, even though it is rarely touted as a major contributor to success.

I didn't wait to get to know people. As soon as I arrived I began to ask all of the teachers and principals I worked with to please invite me to their special events. I served as a guest reader, shared my career paths and clapped vigorously at the end of hundreds of read-arounds, plays, poetry readings, songs, dances, and various other student performances.

These interactions with the students, staff, and principals made my job of working to improve curriculum, instruction, and assessment a joy. I delivered a message to everyone that I cared about his or her work and valued his or her efforts. I also looked through the lens of a central office administrator and saw the familiar disappointment on faces of the principals and the staff when the superintendent or other invited administrators didn't show up for important events. Everyone knew the events were great no matter who was there to witness them, but they were still sad that all of those "other people" didn't come to affirm the greatness.

When I accepted a position as a superintendent, I knew how important "showing up" would be to my success and to the success of the organization. Sure enough, in less than one year, I established a reputation as a superintendent who liked to visit classrooms, who came to special events during the day, in the evenings, and on the weekends. Individual teachers discovered that if they sent me an invitation, I would make every effort to be there.

Now, while visiting schools, I always ask principals and staff members how I can help them do their jobs better. The most common response is to keep coming back to observe them at work. When strolling through classrooms for informal visits, I want teachers to carry on with whatever they are doing when I enter the room. These informal visits yield rich data about the curriculum and how it is being delivered, the teacher's style and the interest and enthusiasm of the students. When possible, I ask students the standard questions and the answers tell me more about the classroom: What are you doing? Why are you doing this? What do you do when you are finished?

At least once during the year, I ask each principal to walk and talk through the classrooms with me. This gives me an opportunity to discuss how the principal is coaching and assessing the professional development of the staff. We also talk about leadership activities and challenges, the budget, the facilities, the grounds, equipment and any other factors that influence the daily life of the school. My goal is to listen, to provide encouragement and feedback and to suggest ideas for future consideration. I have done classroom visits with the president of the teachers' association and found it to contribute greatly to our communication and relationship when working on difficult problems.

This commitment to showing up has also caused me some challenges. In April of my first year as superintendent, I was ill one evening and I missed an open house at an elementary school. The next day I got a call from the principal asking me if I was mad at them. They expected me to be there, because I always showed up. I have learned to call if I am not coming.

"Little Things Mean a Lot" was a popular song in the 1970s. Little does one know how significant "little things" are.

Establishing and Reinforcing District Priorities

"If everything is a priority, then nothing is a priority."

I have always believed that if everything is a priority, then nothing is a priority. Therefore, attempting to practice what I believe, I began a process in my first year as superintendent to work with the governing board to have them identify yearly district priorities. This became an annual event and led to district level, department level and school level goals, objectives, activities, and evaluation measurements all tied in to these district priorities.

The beginning step in the process occurred during the superintendent-board retreat. Although the question of when to conduct such a retreat varies based on a multitude of factors, I found it ideal to have it in mid-March. My rationale was:

- Data as to how we were progressing were available
- Employee evaluations were almost complete
- Time existed to complete follow-up before the beginning of the next year
- Budget planning for the next year was underway, but not yet finalized

What follows is a condensed version of the overall process. In the thirteen years I used the process, it varied only slightly.

Prior to the retreat I sent a memo to the board asking them to identify between two and four district priorities for the next year. I also requested a brief rationale for their choice. Upon receipt of all of these, I had my secretary compile a master list. This was sent to the board prior to the retreat, when the meeting agenda was distributed.

To prepare myself for the retreat, I met with my cabinet. This was composed of assistant superintendents, directors, administrative assistant and three principals representing K–5, 6–8, and 9–12 levels. We did three major things. First, we came to consensus on which of the board-proposed priorities we felt were appropriate and why. Second, we identified additional priorities and the rationale for them. Last, we forecast a price tag for all the priorities.

Very often more than one meeting was required to accomplish these preparation tasks. After these meetings I would determine whether to invite any cabinet members to attend the retreat. This decision was made on a variety of factors—including whether I had enough information so I could facilitate the retreat. Politics always played an essential factor. As an example, one year a director had been frequently criticized by the board. I thought that he would "shine" during the retreat especially because he was responsible for 75% of the areas that had been proposed as district priorities, and he did.

The retreat itself usually lasted two or two-and-a-half days depending on the length of the agenda and how many district priorities had been proposed. It was always my intent to have no more than six priorities, preferably four. However, this result was not always achieved.

During the retreat, before reviewing the board proposed priorities, I would spend an hour sharing my view of the "State of the District." This set the tone for the beginning talk about district priorities. It was extremely revealing to hear each individual board member share their choice for priorities and why. This was the time when special interests or personal agendas would surface. Depending on the number of proposed priorities, this part of the agenda could last between four and six hours.

After thorough discussion, I asked the board to prioritize all proposals. Usually this eliminated several priorities when less than a majority felt the priority had merit. My role in this section was to facilitate the process, being sure that all board members had equal time and to give the board additional information. Also, I provided the financial data for each priority. Next it was my turn to share the cabinet's view of suggested priorities or substitutes. It would be at this time that invited cabinet members would make their presentation. Usually a healthy discussion followed!

The last part of this process was to again have the board prioritize. Consensus was reached ideally when all board members viewed the priority as essential. However, there were many times when board members used their personal lobbying skills to persuade others to change their mind on a previously less desirable priority. These were educational exchanges to say the least!

The identification of district priorities by the board set in motion a cycle of internal communication which ultimately led to the creation of action plans. These were targeted, focused written documents that linked all district-level departments and schools to the district priorities.

Finally, to truly operationalize district priorities and action plans, an accountability system was built into the process. Using the district organizational chart as a guide, all administrators were responsible for monitoring progress of action plans toward completion. This became a component of the evaluation of all administrators, including the superintendent.

ORGANIZING FOR ACTION: WORD FOR THE YEAR

"My overall message was . . . we can be a diamond-quality school district."

July 1, 1989, was to be a significant date in the history of the school district. It was the "official" first day of our newly unified school district. In this case, the new district evolved from a K–8 district's merger with a 9–12 high school district. I was the superintendent of the previous K–8 school district and had recently been appointed by the newly elected K–12 governing board as superintendent of the new district. To say that politics were running high would be an understatement. I had a great personal need to start off the year with everything just right.

I decided to use the beginning-of-the-year district-wide meeting as a vehicle to set the tone for the year and let all employees get a sense of who I was, what I expected, and what views I had about our new school district. During my speech, I wanted to share what I referred to as our "Word for the Year." I was looking for a word to highlight the value of all employees, motivate everyone to do and be their best, reinforce the idea that when working together we are much stronger and more effective than when we do our own thing, and to make everyone realize what a good district we were capable of becoming.

After much deliberation, I chose the word: Diamond. During my presentation, I used a word to represent each letter:

D=Discipline
I =Initiative
A=Accountability
M=Motivation
O=Opportunity
N=New superintendent's expectations
D=Dedication

My overall message was: each of you is a diamond-quality person, and through our focused, collective efforts we can be a diamond-quality school district.

Throughout the year, a diamond symbol appeared on all district-wide newsletters. Each superintendents' message reflected the diamond-quality theme. Our public relations person created a diamond graphic, using all of the word descriptors. This was distributed to all departments and schools.

I used this graphic during my first PTA council meeting to communicate our district-wide focus on quality. It was also shared with the Chamber of Commerce, city council, service clubs, and at all events where I felt it appropriate.

As the year progressed, I began to see evidence that the diamond was a reality. It would appear on teachers' bulletin boards, as part of classroom and school awards programs and many other events. I believed that my main role was to frequently talk about diamond-quality behavior. As an example, at every administrative meeting I would teach or describe a management practice that was, in my opinion, diamond quality. I would also give examples of behaviors or acts that I had personally observed that were reflective of this quality.

It became very natural and very easy to focus on diamond-quality behaviors. I always believed the most important role of a leader is to consistently strive to model behavior that will have a positive and long-lasting impact on the total organization.

Finally, in an effort to create a more permanent reminder of the diamond symbol, I had a lapel pin designed in the diamond shape, surrounded by the name of the school district. This pin became a source of pride to be worn by employees.

Each year I have developed a district "Word for the Year." This word has been communicated at the beginning-of-the-year kick-off meetings and has been put on district-wide internal memos and all publications. It serves as a reminder of what our focus is. Teachers use this theme in classrooms, and district departments have visual reminders throughout their work environment. Some of these words through the years have been words like Team, Glue, Together, Gold, Personal Best, Commitment, Hustle, Plus, Focus, Results, and Expectations.

BUILDING CAPACITY AND CEMENTING RELATIONSHIPS

Communicating with Unions
"We worked as a team, not as a 'we and they.'"

As the new superintendent, my first encounter with the teachers' union was surprising. They informed me that they had gone to impasse six out of the last seven years on contract negotiations and expected to do it again.

After meeting with them a few times I understood why they felt this way. There was no trust between the union and the district. The union believed that the district was not truthful with the numbers and they were right. Actual budget information was not shared with the union.

During my first two months in the district I brought the budget to the union and showed them what we had and ways we might fund the raise they were requesting. By thoroughly reviewing the budget details together we were able to agree to a three-year contract with no financial reopeners for two years. This ended the pattern of declaring impasse and established a new foundation for all future negotiation sessions.

During the next two years the district and union worked together to review the total contract, rewriting and adding new language. These two years gave us a chance to get to know each other on a different level. We worked as a team, not as a "we and they." Subcommittees composed of union and district personnel worked together and presented the recommendations to the whole team. The team then reviewed the language and made changes as needed prior to approval.

The end of the two years was the beginning of bad financial times in the state. The district did not receive a cost-of-living adjustment and had to make major cuts. Because of the work we had done together over the prior two years, the union worked with the district to determine the cuts and settled for no salary increase, allowing the district to maintain a ten-percent reserve. Without developing an open, honest relationship where everyone had the same information, this would never have happened.

Giving a Boost

"I judged this person as needing this morale boost, and I was determined to provide it."

In our organizations there are wonderful people who, in order to remain productive, contributing members of the management team, need a supportive boost. These individuals are often middle managers, principals and district-level support staff. As busy leaders we are, at times, tempted to dismiss their needs and believe that if they "can't stand the heat they should get out of the kitchen." This is a sentiment that should be short-lived. As we experience the peaks and valleys of life as administrators, most of us find that we need support. Sometimes the superintendent is the only person who can provide that extra boost to move a person to the next level of confidence.

My opportunity to assist one of my staff members came after he received word that a grant he wrote for technology funding received a low score. He did not blame this failing on the fact he had little or no experience in grant writing, but on the fact he felt that he was a poor writer. When an opportunity to reapply became available, he approached me and asked what we might do to be successful. I read the first draft of his application and suggested he form a committee to gather input. After reviewing the material from this group, we determined the ideas and suggestions from his committee alone could not be formulated into a winning grant application. Since I valued his technical expertise, and his devotion to the district, I agreed to help him write the grant application. He was delighted. Now as one might imagine, I had little time to devote to this project, but I judged this person as needing this morale boost, and I was determined to provide it. Evening after evening we poured over the guidelines and I edited the work. The process was exhausting.

When I saw the look on his face and the spirit that returned to his demeanor when he learned our grant would be funded, every hour spent was clearly worthwhile. After this news, it was time for me to bow out. He could take it from there. He would now have funds to purchase the desired equipment to support staff development and evaluation services. I knew that this experience would boost his morale and energize his future work.

TENDING TO THE PEOPLE BUSINESS

Knowing You Found the Right Person

"Sometimes in this job you can get overwhelmed and wonder why you ever wanted to be a superintendent. But just find one "Bill" for a new principalship and you know exactly why."

We had an opening for an elementary principalship, and I was concerned about finding the right person. The previous principal had been very popular throughout the district, but had left to take a district-level job. An assistant principal at one of the junior highs indicated an interest and came to see me about his chances. He had no elementary background and, in fact, had primarily high school teaching experience. I shared the challenges he would face in the interviews. I was skeptical about his ability to learn all he would need to know in the six to eight weeks before the interviews would occur.

Interview time arrived and I sat in on the first round as an observer. Bill had clearly done his homework, and he was selected by the panel as a finalist. The final candidates interviewed with me, the assistant superintendent for personnel, and a board member. We were so impressed with what he had done to prepare, how he responded and his genuine desire to do the job. We decided to make the offer. I contacted his principal to let him know and then went to see Bill.

I drove to his office at the junior high and found him working at his desk. I stood at the door and, when he looked up, I could see the nervous smile. I know he was not sure why I was there—to deliver good news or bad news. I simply said, "How would you like to be the principal of Lemon School?" His grin grew to huge proportions. After a few minutes of grinning in sheer delight and breathing hard in surprise, he looked at me and promised, "I will do everything I can to deserve this job and never let you down."

Throughout the first year, I don't think he ever stopped grinning. I attended many events at the school, and his popularity was evident. We had many thoughtful discussions during the year, and I found him to be an enthusiastic learner, willing to talk about the challenges and his joy in the job.

In his second year, I see tremendous positive changes in the school. He is still smiling. The staff, parents and students love him. His smile is tinged with more wisdom and confidence. Every day, I know I made the right choice. His commitment and desire to do a great job have been a joy to watch.

Personnel Evaluation: Giving Honest Feedback

"Giving and receiving feedback in a constructive and timely manner can be a cornerstone of a continuously improving and successful organization."

We are a small district and the superintendent evaluates all principals. The previous superintendent had used an instrument with a numerical scale on which he and the principals rated various items. When I reviewed this with the principals, it was evident that they did not find it particularly valuable for their professional growth. Working together, we rewrote the criteria and developed a narrative format for the evaluation.

As my first year came to an end, I completed the written evaluations. They were time-consuming but honest and thorough. The reactions of the principals were interesting.

In the evaluation conference to discuss them, I provided comments on the principals' strengths and areas in which I perceived they could do better. While they previously indicated a desire for feedback, the principals were somewhat stunned by the suggestions for change or improvement. Two of my strongest principals were amazed about some of my perceptions. It was apparent that no one had ever suggested areas for improvement to them, even though many suggestions reflected common views regarding their leadership. Despite their surprised reactions, the principals appreciated the honest feedback.

For the first time they experienced an evaluation process that contributed to their professional development. It also gave me an opportunity to model the quality of the evaluations I hoped they would provide for their own staff members.

Dealing with a Moral Issue

"The contents of the 'test' contained what any informed person would consider racist, sexist and vulgar references."

Superintendents are increasingly called upon to understand and address issues of diversity. This task is all the more difficult when we find there is not a consensus in our community, our state, or our nation about how to make the phrase "E Pluribus Unum" a reality. Many of us encounter differing points of view concerning such wedge issues as immigration, affirmative action, bilingual education, and Ebonics (a nonstandard English dialect) on a daily basis.

An illustration of the dilemma regarding Ebonics occurred in my district where African-Americans made up less than 6% of the student population. Like most other superintendents in California, I was not contemplating a discussion of Ebonics. I was, nonetheless, forced to find some type of response to the concerns about this issue when a northern California district attempted to apply for a federal bilingual education grant and claimed that Ebonics was "genetically based." The resulting fallout from this unfortunate phrase was visited upon my district a few weeks after the initial media reaction.

One spring afternoon two of my assistant superintendents came to my office with very serious expressions and a sealed envelope. The assistant superintendent assigned to supervise principals looked especially concerned and asked that I wait to read the contents of the envelope until the end of the work day as he knew that I would be disturbed. They then recounted an incident that had occurred in the employee lounge of an elementary school.

Apparently, a contract counselor, a young African-American woman from a local nonprofit social-work agency, overheard three teachers and the principal laughing and kidding about a so-called "Ebonics test" someone had printed from the Internet. At the time of the incident, there were no African-American teachers employed at the school, where about 2% of the students were African-American. The counselor called a local civil rights organization and her supervisor to lodge a formal complaint against the district and the employees involved in the incident. The assistant superintendent from the personnel division commented that if the incident did occur, each person involved, at minimum, should receive a written reprimand. Since there were allegations of discrimination, I asked the director of administrative services to conduct an immediate investigation.

At the end of the day, I opened the envelope and the contents did, in fact, make me feel angry and disappointed. The contents of the "test" contained racist, sexist, and vulgar references. Since the assistant superintendents had heard that items such as the one about Ebonics were retrieved from the Internet, I was anxious to determine the extent of the circulation of such matter. I called principals to alert them to the position in which this placed the district and them as site administrators if they did not put an immediate end to circulation of this type of material. Some admitted to seeing the material and asking that it not be distributed.

The principal at the school involved was the last principal called, and she seemed very nervous. When we met face to face, I asked her under what circumstances would a principal in this district allow a document with such vulgar, racist and sexist language to be circulated in a district facility and joked about in an overtly public way. She began to cry and apologized profusely, indicating she felt caught up in the moment of being friendly with a few teachers and the popular climate regarding public jokes about Ebonics.

Following our conversations, the principal outlined a plan of self-improvement she would immediately undertake. I agreed this would be the most prudent course of action if she intended to remain a principal in our district. Later, I was involved in several conversations with the executive director of the external social-work agency and with the executive director of the civil rights organization. I assured them both that the district would handle the situation appropriately and discussed the district's plan of action.

Beyond this incident that took just a few short minutes in a staff lounge, it was evident I must be involved in numerous follow-up conversations. After the investigation, two assistant superintendents also were immersed in several conferences. In addition, the counselor requested and was granted a transfer to another school. Every principal received a confidential memorandum regarding the incident outlining their liability as site administrators. The memo also reminded them of the obligation a leader faces whenever people are engaged in public ridicule of a person or group.

This episode, while unpleasant and time consuming, gave me an opportunity to remind the administrative staff of their responsibility to be sensitive to issues of diversity, their responsibility for preserving a climate of ethical and moral conduct and, finally, their responsibility for stepping up to the plate to censure unprincipled behavior no matter what the popular climate may dictate.

The Big Principal Switch

"As expected, the principals did not embrace the idea of moving and neither did their communities."

Each day we hope the decisions we make are the right ones for our students. We make them for the right reasons, but not all constituencies agree.

A few years ago I realized that two of our schools were not performing as well as they could. One school had low test scores but a high sense of community in which parents felt very welcomed. The other school had high test scores, but parents and community members did not feel embraced. In looking at what made the difference I discovered the principals of each school reflected the culture of that school. What I did not know was whether the principals caused it or if they had inherited and just continued to maintain the culture.

After spending time with each principal, I determined that one principal was more academic and less community oriented. The other principal was more community oriented and less academic. Each leader did reflect the culture of the school, but they also contributed to the problems.

Hoping to better utilize their skills and to effect change for the students at the two schools, I decided to switch the two principals. As any superintendent who has recommended principal transfers knows, you take some risks when you do this, even though it is the right thing to do. As expected, the principals did not embrace the idea of moving and neither did their school communities.

Board meetings became challenging with supporters of each principal attending and letting the board and me know why the transfers were not a good idea. The board supported my recommendation, and the transfers occurred.

As the principals settled into their new schools, interesting things began to happen. The principals found they liked their new schools. In fact, they realized that their skills could be better utilized. In less than a year the school that was less community oriented began to open up to the community. The community responded by becoming more involved while the school continued to maintain its high academic level.

The school with lower academic standards began looking at what they were doing. They began planning how to improve instruction and how to hold themselves and their students accountable while maintaining great community spirit.

Three years have passed since the move, and my expectations have been more than met. The principals and the schools are thriving. Both schools have become better places for students. A match was made between the principals' skills and the needs of the schools.

KEEPING AN EYE ON THE FUTURE

Blame or Aim: Getting There Together

In our district, we learned two phrases from a consultant: "Blame Frame" and "Aim Frame." The behavior of the "Blame Frame" operator consistently raises two questions: What is wrong? Who is to blame? In contrast, the "Aim Frame" operator asks: "What is our goal? How can we get there together? Often this simple concept can be effectively applied to conflicting staff members and parents.

In numerous situations, I have interjected the concept during an emotional discussion and raised the question, "We can choose the frame we want to operate within: which frame are you choosing?"

On one occasion, a set of angry parents demanded that I take disciplinary action against a teacher and principal who they felt had humiliated their child. They were not sending their child to school until their demand was met. It was a difficult effort to shift the focus from blame and punishment of the adults involved to identifying and supporting their child's needs. However, the Aim Frame approach was effective in moving to a child-centered resolution rather than adult-centered.

Usually, when emotional adults are given venting opportunities and acknowledgment of their feelings, it is much easier to move from the past and present and into the future. Another example where this concept has been utilized is the school staff meeting where all the reasons for maintaining the status quo and not changing are clearly articulated. We are all very familiar with the stories of poor students, no family support, limited English, ineffective administrators, inadequate materials, too many rules and regulations, etc., which are vivid descriptions of why students are not learning. Again, it has been helpful to refocus the group with the question "Are we operating in the Aim Frame or the Blame Frame?"

Generally, the role of the superintendent is to encourage everyone to ask questions directed at identifying goals and next steps: What are we trying to accomplish? What is our purpose or goal?

Future Leaders Program

> "I continued to hear complaints from the teaching staff that I was not promoting people from within the organization."

During my first year as superintendent of a medium-sized, rural school district, I had the opportunity to seek several new certificated administrators. I selected from outside the district an assistant superintendent of learning, a director of special education/student services, a director of alternative education, and a high school vice principal. From inside the district I promoted people to the positions of assistant superintendent of human resources, middle school principal, director of special projects, and elementary school principal. All of these people came to their positions with previous administrative experience.

During the years when these changes were taking place, I continued to hear complaints from the teaching staff that I was not promoting people from within the organization. This was not true. However, the perception existed and needed to be addressed. In fact, only two teachers with many years of classroom experience but no administrative experience nor strong leadership roles outside of the classroom ever applied for any of these vacancies.

In my fourth year of service in this district, I talked to a former superintendent who was responsible for managing the administrative credential program at a nearby university. She was also a lecturer at the local university and was interested in developing a future leaders program with me. My goal was to reach out to those interested in becoming administrators or to those who were already pursuing a credential and to provide experience and some hands-on opportunities in their own district. It would also provide me with an opportunity to get to know and support teachers who were pursuing their first administrative positions. For my university colleague, it was an opportunity to become more closely involved with a school district and perhaps attract future students. And of course for the two of us it promised to be a low-stress, highly rewarding way to share ideas and to make an impact on future leaders.

To recruit participants I asked principals to discuss the program at a faculty meeting and to seek out any strong candidates that might be interested. I wrote a description of the program, limited the number of people to eight, clarified that there would be no remuneration or promises of future positions and requested that interested individuals write me a letter.

I was delighted to receive letters from nine people. My colleague and I prepared a general outline of four seminar sessions. We spent one session giving each of the eight people selected an opportunity to talk about themselves, their prior schooling, and their professional experiences. We invited the Assistant Superintendent of Human Resources to come in and talk about recruiting administrators and the process and criteria for selection. She brought several handouts that listed knowledge and skills as they applied to the administrative role. I talked about some of my own experiences as a principal and district office administrator prior to taking the job as superintendent.

Not everyone in the group said they wanted to seek administrative positions. Three of the participants were completing an administrative credential program at a local university together. They shared insights about their classes and the materials they were reading. Everyone, however, agreed that while these discussions made them more aware of what the principals at their schools were doing, they all needed more hands-on experience to be more informed about the role of administrator.

At the fourth session, we agreed to schedule individual appointments with each participant so that they could discuss their personal and professional goals with us. Then we would seek a current administrator to be their mentor during the coming school year. This matching would be connected as closely as possible to their goals and would broaden their base of experience to prepare them for a future administrative position.

In the following two years, four members of the intern group were promoted within the district. One was assigned as a district level resource teacher to work on a five-year federal grant and another was assigned to a middle school as a counselor.

Later, one was hired as an elementary school principal, one was assigned as a high school dean and the counselor was moved to director of alternative programs. We demonstrated through this program that we listened to concerns and valued our current employees. I didn't hear any further concerns from staff about why we didn't hire from the inside!

Leaving a Legacy

> "A legacy is built by having clear principles and standards based on deeply held beliefs and then staying true to each one."

If each of us left our schools and/or school districts better than we found them, we would be making a significant contribution. To me this means creating programs of value, establishing an ethic of fair and just human relations, and institutionalizing a focus on teaching and learning throughout the organization.

Constancy of purpose is critical for the long-term positive direction of a school and district. Too often we move from one initiative to another without connecting our actions to a whole, losing the constancy and a sense by others that we have a common purpose.

Strategic planning is a good way to focus an organization. While there are various models, they all involve spending concentrated time with representatives of groups who care about learning and will work to set a clear direction based on deeply held and shared beliefs. Once a mission, vision, and beliefs are set, they must be consistently articulated and presented. They must form the basis of each and every decision so people making decisions and those carrying them out understand they are contributing to a sustained effort.

When I became superintendent in my first district, we had mission and belief statements in place. However, I wanted a way to consistently communicate our beliefs in a succinct manner so that all our actions could be tied to our central mission. I developed four themes built on the mission and beliefs. Those four themes became the basis of my formal and informal talks with staff, parents, and the community. The themes also became the anchor points for all my writing, including my newsletter to staff and my weekly columns in the local newspaper. The goal was for people to know, without a doubt, what mattered to our school district.

At the beginning of my first year as superintendent, in the kick-off meeting with the leadership team and their support staff, I shared the four themes: Improved Student Learning, Caring and Commitment, Efficiency and Effectiveness, and Teamwork. I described each one and gave examples from their schools that exemplified the themes at a high level.

From that first day, the leadership team members addressed those themes in their work at each school. They shared the themes and what they meant with their staffs, students, and parents. The yearly goals of each principal were organized under the themes, and their work products reflected their focus on them.

At the beginning of my second year at the leadership team kick-off gathering, I started by putting on the overhead the themes from our first year. Then I told everyone I would next share the themes for the coming year. When the same four themes appeared on the screen, the result was laughter and applause. My explanation for the same four themes was that what we stand for does not change. Our methods to achieve our goals may change, but our commitment to principles does not change.

People still in the district today can recite the themes. A legacy is built by having clear principles and standards based on deeply held beliefs and then staying true to each one. We should understand the importance of purpose and how it can leave a powerful legacy.

LESSONS LEARNED

- Reinforce your interest by remembering to observe and honor all levels of the organization.
- Don't assume: listen first.
- Be sensitive to the difference between positional and personal power.
- Affirm the work of all staff and students by being visible at school events.
- Determine the needs of the organization by creating a process which identifies needs and priorities.
- Use visual reminders such as a word or a phrase to serve as an external method for communicating values.
- Support through tangible methods rather than merely a pep talk.
- Recognize the importance of honest feedback, an important component for personal growth.
- Develop internal training programs to recruit new administrators.
- Do what's important to keep your organization moving forward.
- Use the consensus process for decisions impacting the majority of employees.
- Develop an organizational chart that communicates the message about institutional priorities and relationships.
- Keep your organization's time zones in perspective. Honor the *past*, be cognizant of *present* priorities, and share a clear vision of the *future*.
- Take immediate corrective action when basic principles of fairness and positive human relations are violated.

- Allow people to learn from their mistakes.
- Model ethical and moral conduct as an ongoing responsibility of a leader.
- Cultivate a reputation as a fair, ethical and proactive leader; the dividends for your organization are incalculable.
- Maintain constancy of purpose.

Chapter 4

Knowing Your Students

"First, we should never lose sight of our students. Second, we never fully know what it takes to touch a child. Finally, we must be careful with our power to ensure that we influence students positively."

Without exception, we went into education because we care for young people and because we believe we can make a difference for them. Our caring for students is what got us going, what keeps us going, and what provides us our ultimate job satisfaction.

As leaders and teachers, we work hard to connect with students, to motivate them, and to be their champions. As continuous learners, we are intrigued and energized by our students, amazed at their talents and points of view, cheered by their spirit, and inspired by their lives.

MOTIVATING YOUNG PEOPLE

The DARE Graduation: Setting Goals

During the annual round of end-of-year ceremonies held throughout the district, I usually walk into an event, glance at the program, and discover that I am expected to give the welcome address or introduce a special guest. Occasionally, however, I am surprised to discover that I am expected to be the keynote speaker.

For example, at a Drug Abuse Resistance Education (DARE) graduation ceremony held for nearly 200 seventh graders at a middle school,
the young police officer who had planned the program told me I was the
keynote speaker. He asked if I could speak for about ten minutes and
said he did not have anything specific he would like me to talk about.

As I took my seat, I started rifling through my brain for topics that a
roomful of seventh graders would find appealing on an especially
beautiful springtime afternoon. I partially listened to the officer as he
gave a brief overview of the DARE curriculum he taught to the students, introduced and thanked the principal and the teachers for their
support, and he introduced a few more dignitaries. Then it was time
for me to speak.

As I approached the podium, I decided that goal setting, a topic
highlighted in the officer's presentation, would be pertinent to the students' lives. I looked into the auditorium of squirming, rustling seventh graders and knew they were antsy to get their certificates. I had to
be brief and interesting.

I structured my comments on stories from my own past as a student.
I began with a story from seventh grade. A friend of mine went on a
family vacation to Niagara Falls and I was so jealous because my family never traveled to any tourist-type places. My mother worked in a
clothing factory assembling clothes, and my stepfather worked as a
horse ranch groom. They both worked hard, but we could barely afford
to visit relatives who lived only several hours away. I yearned to travel
and I continued my presentation with another story. In ninth grade, my
best friend's family went by airplane to Disneyland and stayed at the
Disneyland Hotel for a week. Once again, I was so envious, but knew
that such an incredibly expensive trip was beyond my family's resources. California was very high on my list of dream travel destina-
tions. As my presentation came to a close, I concluded with a final
story. In eleventh grade, my Spanish class took a trip to Mexico and I
was the only student who could not afford the $300 cost of the trip.
Devastated, I could not join my classmates. Sometime during the year,
I decided to find a way to change my life. I was determined to be able
to travel anywhere in the world.

As I looked at the audience, I noticed they were quiet and listening.
Most of the students at this school came from families eligible for the
free or reduced lunch program. I guessed that few of them had probably ever taken any fancy vacations either.

I focused my closing remarks on the importance of goal setting. I encouraged students to set small goals each day and to never lose sight of them. I talked about going to community college while working full-time to support myself, pursuing a bachelor's degree and starting to work as a teacher, working full-time as a teacher, being a mother and wife while pursuing a master's degree, working as a principal, and deciding to get my Ph.D. so I could become a superintendent and find ways to improve schools.

At this point, you could have heard a pin drop in the room. The students waited for the punch line. Where did I go on vacation? When I told the students about my trip to Spain to see the beautiful places pictured in my old high school Spanish book, they broke out in spontaneous applause. As I shared travels with my own children throughout North and South America, the students applauded more.

My seventh-grade audience understood the importance of setting goals and knew that I was sharing a real-life example from my heart. It was a memorable moment for them and me.

Continuation High Schools Get a Bad Rap

Right or wrong, continuation high schools often have bad reputations. The students are considered losers, the teachers mediocre, and the principal in a dead-end job. In this age of accountability, their test scores often reinforce the image. These are unfair assumptions in far too many cases.

Every year as I participate in the graduation ceremonies for our continuation high school, I realize how fortunate our students are to have this opportunity. Students are not all the same; they do not all learn in the same way. Benson School makes it a priority to ensure that students there receive the best education and best preparation for their futures.

The principal sets very high expectations for behavior and performance. Staff members know every student. Teachers collaborate on lessons and instruction. They are creative in their work and take a personal interest in their students. Parents feel welcomed and supported, despite their usual trepidation about having their students in a "continuation" high school. And the students love the school—a big accomplishment for them.

At a recent Benson graduation, all of this came home to me through two graduating seniors and six graduates who returned for the ceremony. The six graduates were a delight to see since I had known most of them when they attended Benson. They had been invited back for a unique reason.

The school, through the principal's leadership, had established a foundation that had raised $10,000, a tidy sum for a school of just over 100 students. Each of the six graduates was receiving either a $250 or a $500 scholarship from the foundation to further his or her education. In actuality, each alumnus was already involved in school and not one had a grade point average below 3.0. What a wonderful model for the graduating class—they were seeing the results of staying with their education from graduates of their own school.

The graduating class was represented by two seniors who had been chosen to speak. Maria had been close to dropping out of the comprehensive high school. But here she was giving a commencement speech and being recognized for her leadership and achievement. Maria is articulate and strong. She was selected to serve on the county Human Relations Committee, worked full time, and had plans for college.

Then there was Amy. She stepped to the microphone to speak and to thank the school, the staff and the principal for standing by and supporting her. Amy's dad had been diagnosed with terminal cancer in the fall of that year, and had died just two months shy of graduation. People at the school provided her with alternative ways to get schoolwork done while she helped her mom take care of her dad. She acknowledged that she would not be there if not for Benson. Her strength and accomplishments were evident along with her joy and sweetness. Moist eyes were evident everywhere.

I was so proud at this moment. I was proud of the school, the staff, and their incredible work to help students. And especially proud of the students who were recognized and spoke that night. But I was also proud of our district for creating the kind of school that met the needs of these very special young people.

The Perfect Graduation Story

As each school year comes to a close, I find myself frantically searching for the "perfect graduation story." I believe it is very important for me to deliver a significant message to the graduates of each of our high schools via a story—and the story has to be "perfect" in every way. It has to deliver a clear message, be straightforward and powerful. It cannot insult any religious, racial, ethnic, or any other group who might be in the audience. It needs to be short enough to hold everyone's attention, yet long enough to be a complete story.

I start searching for next year's story as soon as graduation season is over. For the past two years I have spoken at nine graduations in a row and have really come to appreciate the value of having a "perfect" story. It is important that I enjoy the story since I tell it so many times and, in a large urban district, you know that there will be people in the audience who attend more than one graduation. They need to enjoy hearing the story more than once too.

To find the "perfect" story, I leaf through old books on my shelves at home and at the office. I wander through the bookstore and pick up new books in the poetry, philosophy, and literature sections. I read some of the Internet stories that are forwarded to me. And of course, I ask my friends.

The message of last year's story was the value of everyone in a community taking care of each other. This year it was that we all have the opportunity to choose how we see the world. I know that a story was a good one when graduates walk across the stage to shake my hand and whisper, "I really liked your story." I expect the graduates to be so filled with emotion that I am always surprised that they really listened to what I had to say. It makes the search all worthwhile.

THE WAY YOUNGSTERS ENERGIZE US

Arturo's Drawing

I am often known to visit schools for what I call my "kid fix." A "kid fix" is what I need when the job gets to be overwhelming or when I feel buried under the sometimes "crazy adult" things that occur. I have, since becoming an assistant superintendent, often spent time at schools to observe classes, read to kids, or just talk with them. These moments remind me of our greater purpose as educators.

One of the elementary schools in my district is largely Hispanic, quite different from the rest of the schools in the district. I love visiting the campus because visitors always feel welcome. The principal is fun and loves his job, the teachers are wonderful and the kids are a delight to observe. During a visit to this school, the principal and I were walking the campus and enjoying our time visiting classes. Watching students and teachers interact in this school is always special. Their interactions exemplify the joy and excitement of teaching and learning. At recess, I was standing near the playground when a little boy came up to me and handed me a piece of paper. He had drawn a flower on the paper and written, "Dear Dr. Jones . . . Love, Arturo." It was a moment of such sweetness and sincerity that I was truly touched. I thanked him warmly, and he shyly shook my hand. For some unknown reason, I made a positive impression on this young student, and he responded in such a kind way. Since that moment, I saw Arturo on several occasions and a special bond developed between us.

Arturo's simple act reminded me of several lessons critical to the superintendency. First, we should never lose sight of our students. Second, we never fully know what it takes to touch a child. Finally, we must be careful with our power to ensure that we influence students positively.

What's Wrong with Your Face?

During a particularly difficult several months when challenging events caused havoc with my sleep, diet, and exercise patterns, my complexion became very bad. It was red and rough all around my nose and forehead area. I covered it with makeup as best I could and continued about my work.

A regular activity of mine was going to schools, spending time in classrooms and talking with students about what they were doing and why. A special pleasure with elementary children was listening to them read.

One day I crouched next to a first-grade girl who was delighted to read to me. Part way through the story, she turned toward me, looking me directly in the eye, and asked, "What's wrong with your face?"

Slightly taken aback, I answered, "Well, I've had some difficult times lately and my skin seems to have broken out."

"Have you gone to the doctor?" she continued, still staring straight at me. "No, I guess I haven't found time," I confessed. "Well," she said, "you need to."

With that, she returned to her book and completed the story. I thanked her for reading to me and for her advice. As I walked into my office, I told my assistant my first task was to call a doctor about my face. When she asked why it was so urgent, I replied, "When a six-year-old says it needs to be done, you know it does."

The Fingerprint Apron

Everyone gets down from time to time and needs to be heard, but out-and-out whining is my least favorite behavior. My patience is tried most when I hear an adult who works in schools complain, maybe about having to stand crosswalk duty or, worse, the possibility of being assigned to lunchroom duty.

Like all humans, I have my moments. Yet, I learned when I hear a whine creep into my voice, I need some perspective. I jump in my car and head for a school. In one district, I often went directly to the school for the severely physically handicapped children. Although I visited that school on a regular basis, it was the place I went for a reality, or "deal with it," check. Seeing the children always brought me back to what really matters.

On one occasion, I saw a little girl who, for the first time could communicate because a staff person created a board covered with pictures of commonly used items and concepts. The child, who had no oral language, could point to the picture of what she wanted. In her case, the pointing was done with a stick held between her teeth, because she could not use her arms.

Whenever I went the school, the principal would always want to take me to see one particular little boy. He was a four-year-old who the staff were sure they could help speak, despite his parents' hopelessness. Each time we would see the little boy, the principal would say, "Won't you say 'hi' to my boss? It would be really wonderful if you would, because she is a special lady to me." It was easy to see by the light in the boy's eyes that he adored his principal and really wanted to please her. But he'd just smile his winning, ear-to-ear smile and shyly look away. The day he said, "Hi!" I thought the staff would never stop high-fiving—or crying. The messages of the principal's perseverance and his response were clear; there are no limits for any child, and never stop trying.

Over several years, I grew particularly close to and fond of a teenager whom I first met at the comprehensive high school. At that time, he was about six feet tall and a trim, but solid, 160 pounds. Shortly thereafter, cerebral palsy began its destructive march through his body, and eventually he had to attend the special school. The one thing disease could not touch was his glowing smile—one that simultaneously lit up a room and made one's heart sink. As I watched his body shrink and his ability to use his limbs fail him, I marveled at his spirit. He smiled and encouraged his younger, smaller classmates and brought joy to their lives in addition to that of every adult around him. The day he died, I felt an ache I thought would never subside. But then I focused on his brilliant smile, the message he brought everyone when he was alive, and the memory he left us that will never fade.

These three children had in common their struggles with some of life's cruelest challenges, but they also had their beautiful spirits and smiles. At an end-of-the-year ceremony, the children gave me a present, a gift I will treasure always. It is a reminder of the importance of our jobs and why there is no room for whining. The gift is a green apron, covered with fingerprints in the colors of the rainbow—one fingerprint of each child in the school.

BEING A CHAMPION FOR YOUTH

Promotion Program Causes Chaos

Usually a graduation or a promotion ceremony is an event that makes everyone happy—students, parents, teachers and administrators! However, little did I know that one such ceremony would cause an uproar that resulted in the opposite.

The ceremony was a middle school promotion, and because the school had opened only two years earlier, this was the first eighth-grade class to be promoted to high school. The principal was the second one for the school, having been appointed only nine months earlier.

In addition to the typical middle school classes, this school housed three special education classes. These classes were under the direction of the county office of education, but because of space and geographic factors, they were housed at this new middle school. Although teachers of these classes were county employees, they were very much a part of the middle school faculty. A special effort was made to include these students and teachers in all regular school activities.

As far as I was concerned, this school was functioning quite smoothly and had been free of any major problems since its opening. As I looked out at the guests and staff intermingled with all of our governing board members, I was quite pleased and, to a degree, a little smug. The smugness came from the knowledge that despite a very fast construction timeline, this school had been completed in time. Because of the multitude of tasks that had to be completed, there were the usual skeptics who had reservations that all would come together in order to achieve what had been promised.

The promotion ceremony had all of the usual elements: opening remarks, acknowledgments, student speeches, musical entertainment, announcement of class honor students, special awards, etc. The last task before the promotion certificates were distributed was the awarding of special class awards. The staff had decided to honor students who had excelled in math, language arts, science, social studies and physical education. These awards were presented by teachers in their content area.

After the first group of teachers had presented their awards, I noticed a little movement and conversation in the location where the special education students and parents were sitting. As this continued, a nod from the principal (seated on stage) to the assistant principal (standing in the back of the auditorium, but in constant view and eye contact with the principal) resulted in the assistant principal moving to the area of the conversation and movement.

A few minutes later, the assistant principal came to the side of the stage and motioned to the principal. Not long after, a miniconference with the principal, assistant principal, two parents of special education children and a special education teacher took place, once again at the back of the auditorium. As this was going on, the awards continued to be distributed. By now, I was getting several questioning looks from board members. These looks were quite familiar and the translation was, "What's going on and why don't you do something?" By this time, the miniconference had ended, but the parents had not returned to their seats. They were standing where the discussion had taken place. As I expected, the principal now came to the side of the stage and motioned to me.

The principal informed me that the parents of the special education students were furious. First, none of the special education students were receiving the special awards, and second, in the promotion program, the names of these students did not appear in alphabetical order like all the other students, but they were listed separately under the category of Special Education Students. They were demanding that a new program be created. They wanted the "error" corrected by announcing that the special education teachers had made a mistake and had forgotten to identify special education students for the special awards. They demanded the new program to be done NOW and distributed before the promotion ceremony ended! The principal wanted some advice as to how to proceed.

We agreed that a new program would be done. We determined that it could not be done immediately, but it would be sent home to all parents with a letter of explanation. We also decided that no announcement would be made about the special education teachers forgetting the awards during the ceremony. The fact was that the special education teachers had chosen not to participate. The principal shared the plan with the parents, and they left the auditorium for a brief period. The ceremony continued and concluded. The principal informed me that the two parents wanted to meet with me immediately after the ceremony.

Prior to meeting with the parents, I briefed the governing board members and asked that the board president join the meeting with the parents. I also insisted that the principal join us. I instructed the assistant principal to brief the special education teachers on what had occurred and asked them not to discuss the issue at this time.

During the parent meeting, it was clear that the parents were extremely upset and it appeared that nothing would please them. My position was that I believed an error was made with the way the student names were placed in the program but that the teachers did have a choice whether or not to participate in the special awards. At the conclusion of the meeting, the parents stated that they were not at all pleased. They announced their intention to go to the press and to file a series of complaints! The parents did follow through with their plans, and this matter continued for several months. Complaints were filed with the governing board, the state department of education, the county governing board and the federal government. The conclusion of all groups was that the students were not discriminated against, and the matter was finally put to rest.

Internally, several things occurred. The principal met with the special education teachers and with the administrator from the county office of education. It was agreed that there would be exact conformity with the nature of all awards given at future promotion ceremonies. Second, the principal assumed full responsibility for the program problem because she failed to review it before it was sent to the printer.

My personal view was that we had made several errors that never should have occurred. This view was made known to everyone. We acknowledged that all students have the right to be treated equally and certainly should have the right to receive the same honors given to other children. I counseled the principal to review this matter and to identify what steps should be taken to prevent this from happening in the future.

Jose and Alejandro

Julie teaches with total commitment. It always seems to many that her life is her teaching. But I know another side of her that has made her very special in my life.

I had just arrived in the district as a new superintendent over six years ago, when Julie, a single white woman, had adopted two orphan boys from Mexico. Both had physical and intellectual challenges and would demand incredible effort on any parent's part. Yet, here was Julie—not married and living on one teacher's income— trying to make it work.

Alejandro is the oldest. He was withdrawn and appeared to me to be undernourished. The result was a boy who had not developed fully. His language did not seem strong, nor did his body. Jose was much the same, but was even tinier for his age. He clearly was going to have some learning difficulties. While teaching full time, Julie poured her heart into making the best possible life for both boys.

During the next few years, I had the opportunity to know all three of them better; both boys were in special education classes and receiving speech therapy. Their bodies and minds were clearly growing stronger.

Alejandro moved from special education to regular classes by the time he entered third grade. He has been a delight to watch as he stands with his classmates and sings or speaks to audiences. It has been more difficult with Jose. His learning handicaps were more severe and Julie has had a tough time being objective about his needs.

Over the last two years, they have become a true light in my life. They come to see me in my office, and no matter what I am doing, I stop. You see, I have no choice. Jose comes running and jumps into my arms. Alejandro follows more shyly. I get great hugs and tender kisses. Then I get to hear about their activities.

Julie has done a wonderful job of providing them unique opportunities. Both boys have taken violin lessons and both are playing sports. They love books, movies, and, to my delight, me.

Superintendents do not always receive this kind of gift. Jose and Alejandro make me smile and help me know that I can be, and am, important to children. They remind me of why this job is worthwhile. Julie makes me appreciate the incredible strength and commitment that teachers have. I feel humble with them and joyous for knowing this wonderful family.

Andrew

Everyone in school knew Andrew. Kids said, "Andrew's different, but he's okay. He walks a little differently and says some unusual things." The only annoyance was sometimes Andrew's disruptions were ignored when similar behavior by other students would have landed them in the principal's office.

Andrew was okay, because the adults in his life—parents and school staff—took the mystery away. Teachers talked openly with their students about Andrew and his autism. Children rarely point fingers, whisper or giggle about others when they are treated with respect by sharing knowledge. Parents and staff did that; they talked about what we know about autism, answered all the kids' questions, discussed the implications for Andrew and them as his classmates.

This was possible because of the positive relationship developed between the parents and district and school staff. Parents, administrators, teachers and support staff worked together. We learned everything we could about autism, researching strategies developed by leading experts, staying current on the latest developments, and analyzing the implementation, making modifications—for each of our autistic children.

Teachers always rise to the occasion. Although Andrew couldn't sing or follow the lyrics, the music teacher invited him to be part of the school chorus. Andrew never missed class, participating as his attention span allowed. His classmates learned to help or ignore him as appropriate—he was Andrew, a fellow chorus student who did things a little differently.

The culmination of the year was the annual music concert. Andrew's parents were somewhat apprehensive, fearing he might disrupt the concert, bothering the several hundred other parents attending, but the chorus teacher and students were unconcerned. Andrew was part of the chorus, so of course he was going to be part of this program.

That night, Andrew stood on the risers with all the other students. Once in a while he sang a few words, but most of the time he just stood there—but he had learned how to stand quietly and be part of the group without standing out.

During the applause, the students around Andrew congratulated him, and he smiled in return. They were all proud of themselves. So were we, his parents and staff, who clapped, smiled and brushed away the tears running down our cheeks.

Maximizing Connections for Students

Depending upon the reporting structure in a school district, a superintendent may or may not have a great deal of direct contact with principals. In my case one of my major responsibilities was to develop the "organizational chart" and related methods of line and staff relationships. Therefore, I was the evaluator of the principals and had the most direct relationship with them.

In our school district the expectation and practice existed that when a situation arose at a school which was unresolved or resolved but not to the satisfaction of parents, I was to be informed of the circumstances by the school principal.

In one situation, an unresolved concern related to a parent request to retain a third-grade student. By school board policy, following teacher-parent and then teacher-principal-parent discussions, the decision to retain or not was the prerogative of the school principal. In this case, because the student was very bright and the case for retention appeared weak, the principal denied the request for retention. The parents subsequently took their request to the district governing board and I became involved when asked to obtain background information from the parents. Ultimately, I was able to inform the board that the principal had followed the board policy exactly and I was in complete agreement with the principal's decision.

The governing board supported our position to deny retention and asked that I send a letter to the parents indicating the denial. This was done immediately.

Because of my considerable involvement in this situation and my curiosity concerning the outcome of our action, I personally traced the progress of this student from the fourth grade through high school graduation.

It was the parent's original contention that because of the physical size and stature of their child, which was less than that of his classmates, he would become intellectually and developmentally handicapped. This turned out to be completely erroneous; in fact, he made excellent personal and academic progress to the degree that he was accepted for entrance into a very prestigious private college. Needless to say, I was most proud of his accomplishments and was thrilled to note at the district's scholarship foundation's presentation that he received three financial scholarships totaling $1,500.

The day following the presentations I went to the high school to thank his English teacher for all of the personal and professional encouragement she had given him. She informed me that this young man's parents had separated and that a lack of financial resources was a major obstacle facing the student. The English teacher cared so much that she had supplied the white shirt and tie he had worn to the scholarship presentation. While I was talking to the teacher, her eyes filled with tears and she told me that the scholarship money was not enough. Although the student did qualify for a partial college scholarship which would pay for his housing, his parents could not supply the money for books and tuition. I thought to myself that there must be some way to get further help, and there was!

At that time I was a very active member of our local Rotary Club and was currently serving my last month as its president. As luck would have it, we had one more executive board meeting before the end of my tenure as president. We had several successful fund-raising events, and as I reviewed the June financial summary, it was clear that we would exceed our projected financial carryover to the next year. Here was my opportunity to merge my community/service club leadership role with my superintendent/advocate-for-children role.

Since one of the club priorities that year was to increase the club contribution to the high school scholarship foundation, I prepared very purposefully for the last Rotary board meeting. When the time was appropriate, I made a request that the club allocate enough money to cover books and tuition for this student. A fairly lengthy discussion occurred which included other Rotarian requests for use of this "newly found" money. When the vote came, my request was unanimously approved with two stipulations:

- the money would go directly from the Rotary treasury to the college with specifications for its use, and
- the student would provide the Rotary Club with quarterly academic progress reports.

To my delight, the club indicated that this support would continue throughout the student's four-year college career as long as he continued to progress satisfactorily and meet the two stipulations.

In retrospect, I am gratified that I took personal interest and pride in the success of this student, especially since both the principal and I had greatly displeased his parents by denying their retention request. I also felt satisfaction in demonstrating the value of community/service club involvement in providing a personal connection for an individual student's continuing education and hopefully, a contribution to a full, productive life.

CONNECTING WITH STUDENTS

Growing Tall

One of the wonderful things about being a superintendent in a small district is the chance to get to know students and families. You see students when you grocery shop and when you attend school events. I have always found that kids are the big motivators in the work I do.

When I first came to this small district, I met a young boy who was student body president during his eighth grade year. He was about 5'5" tall with blond/brown hair. Jack's smile was large and he was clearly "a man about campus." But besides being well liked, Jack was a kind, poised young man who did well academically. His mom was a teacher at the school and her pride was always evident.

Over the next four years, I watched Jack grow. From the small 5'5" cute eighth grader, I saw a 6'6" lean basketball player develop and blossom. It was rewarding to observe the changes through his high school years. He stayed active in sports and leadership activities, was popular with other students and was appreciated by the staff. I recall a few times when I would go to the high school and see Jack out on campus, surrounded by friends.

When graduation came that year, I made some remarks about having had the chance to watch the students in the class for five years. I acknowledged the wonderful things they had done and how much they had changed over the five years since I had first met them. I then shared with the audience that I knew they were aware of how much they had grown up and mentioned one young man who had been a small eighth grader. I talked about how he had matured into this outstanding varsity basketball player and how much fun I had watching him over the years. I had no idea whether he or the audience would know whom I was talking about.

During the awarding of the diplomas, Jack came through the line where I was shaking hands and he gave me a hug. After the ceremony, I was standing to the side when Jack came up to me and said, "Thank you! I know you were talking about me, and it meant a lot."

I realized from this small incident that I can make a difference by caring about the kids and was reminded one more time of why I do this job. The look of joy and appreciation on his face said it all—it mattered that I knew and thought about him. That is what we are all about.

School as a Safe Haven

Eddie was a difficult kid. In fourth grade, he had a streetwise sense beyond his years. He was very much on his own in life. Being raised by a single-parent father, he was often on the playground well into the evening. Dad was an enlisted man at the nearby base, but he was often home late. If he did make it home early, he spent the first few hours drinking. The interactions between father and son were abrupt or nonexistent. The whole school worried about Eddie, but as the site principal, I worried more.

He was continually in playground scrapes with other kids. I received fairly constant calls from local merchants who asked me if I couldn't do something about his neighborhood loitering since they could never reach the father. He asked people for money, and if he was given some, he bought candy. He received free lunches at school, and we all knew that it was probably his only meal of the day. Teachers would let him work in their classrooms after school doing little odd jobs to keep him occupied. We continually sought out activities for him, recognizing his potential.

One evening around ten, I received a call from the base informing me that Eddie's father had fallen two stories from a large scaffold and was badly injured. He wasn't expected to live. I had developed a relationship with his next-door neighbor because of all the problems we had experienced and I called to alert her. She already knew. Another serviceman had stopped by the house on his way home. The neighbor assured me that Eddie was in good hands and that he would spend the night with them before they took him to the hospital in the morning.

I couldn't sleep that night. I got up early and pulled into the school parking lot around 6:30 a.m. As I walked up the long cement walkway to the school entryway, I saw a scrunched-up body by the door, tucked behind some bushes. It was Eddie. He was shivering and in tears. I leaned down to him, and he told me that he had left the neighbor's house before they woke up. He told me he wanted to come to school "because it's the only safe place I know." I just fell apart.

For all the challenges, the struggles, and the tough-love talks Eddie experienced at school, he still felt safe. He received guidance, discipline, food, shelter, and love. He drove us crazy at times, but we saw such hope in such a desperate young man. And here he was, with a father on the brink of death, reaching out to his school as his only safe haven.

Eddie's dad passed away early in the morning that day and the entire community embraced Eddie in his loss. No relatives were ever discovered, and a local family of five took Eddie in as part of their family within a week. After a year, he was officially adopted. I kept track of Eddie for several years and on into high school. Each year, he became a more successful student. He ran cross-country and he was a celebrated low hurdler. When I moved out of the state, I lost track of him. But he's a part of my soul. As I look at the many students who walk through our classroom doors each fall, I look into their eyes. For many, school is the only safe place they know. We must be mindful and acutely aware of who those students are. They are often disguised as feisty troublemakers, but in their hearts and souls, they are reaching out to just feel safe.

The Honesty of Children

Children are honest and direct. They are quite "no nonsense" about their observations of their worlds. One of my fondest memories of this endearing trait of children occurred in my monthly visit to a first-grade classroom in a district in which I spent three wonderful years.

I love childrens' books. Throughout my career, I have made it a top priority to read wonderful books to students frequently. These visits to classrooms have been highlights of my career. I have encouraged teachers to invite me to their classrooms to share favorite pieces of literature correlated with certain curriculum units or to read stories during special times of the year. I have shared books from my travels and I have recited poetry written by famous poets and creative high school students. No matter what age of child, I am always amazed at how focused and receptive students are to guest readers in the classroom. Children love to listen to adults read . . . they hear, they visualize and they soak in exciting new information from a new voice in the classroom. When I think of my many days of reading to children, I always settle on my day in first grade with George.

Every few months I still exchange letters with George, now a high school student. I have been writing to George for the past several years. We started corresponding when I left my previous district and he wrote me a good-bye letter. When he asked me to write back, I did, and we have continued a letter-writing correspondence ever since. When I first met George, he was in first grade. He was an avid reader. His teacher told me that he voraciously consumed every storybook in the classroom and he visited the community library every week with his mother. He simply loved books! I read to his class often. Each time, he sat right in front of me, oblivious to those around him. He seemed to hang on my every word. He followed my eyes and mouth attentively. He smiled at funny things and became wide-eyed when I began the story line crescendo. Sometimes, I found myself reading just to him— George was my audience within the group of twenty-five children.

On one particular day, George truly seemed enraptured. As I watched him intently, I knew he was loving the story I was reading. He moved his head when I moved mine, and his eyes never left my face. He just loves this story, I thought. When I concluded, I saw him slowly raise his arm up indicating he had something important to share with me. I just knew he was going to ask an in-depth question about what he had just heard. I was ready for him!

He looked at me with big brown eyes, and he said rather emphatically, "You look old!" The teacher choked back a laugh, and so did I! I looked at him and asked him gently, "What do you mean?" He told me quite precisely what he meant as he pointed to the wrinkles around my mouth and around my eyes. "You look old there . . . and there . . . and there!"

I still chuckle when I think of that day. The focused gaze I had observed was actually complete attention to the numerous ways the wrinkles on my cheeks and around my eyes moved as I read with expression. As he watched me that day, I even remember becoming more expressive with each and every word. So funny! After the class moved on to the next activity, George's twenty-something teacher reminded me that his mom was only around twenty-five. I realized that the combined ages of his mom and his teacher, the two most important women in his life, were just about my age and to him, I really did look old! The memory of that day still brings a smile to my face. When I look in the mirror and see those wrinkles myself, I think of them as George's story lines!

In about every other letter, he tells me how he remembers me reading to his class. I know that it meant a lot to him. Some day I'll share this story with him and we'll both have a good laugh. I will remind him how much that little story told me about children. Kids are so direct, honest and forthright, and, unfortunately, quite accurate in their observations! Listen closely to children. They tell it like it is!

When a Student Dies

It is inevitable that with thousands of students enrolled in our schools that a certain numbers of students will die during the school year. Some of them die from chronic illnesses such as leukemia or asthma. Some will die from illnesses that seem to strike them overnight such as influenza. The most traumatic deaths among our students, however, are the unanticipated deaths that shock and surprise us. These deaths are usually caused by accidents or suicides.

This past year four of our students died suddenly without any warning. Their deaths caused students, staff, families, and community members to consider how unfair it is for youngsters who are just beginning their lives to be taken away from their families and others who care about them. It raised questions about why such tragic events happened and what we can do to prevent these events from happening to others. The loss of these students brought youngsters and adults together at our school to support one another and to share their grief.

A middle school student was riding on the back of his father's motorcycle when they were hit by another car. They were both wearing helmets, but they both died instantly. The student was a popular eighth grader who was known by many and was a leader at his school.

A fifth-grade boy was sent to his room by his mother for not doing his chores. He put a belt around his neck, stood on a chair, and hooked it on to the top of his bunk bed. Somehow or other, he fell and couldn't get loose. He died before his mother found him in his room.

An eleventh-grade high school student walked over to his aunt's house after school on a warm spring day. He just planned to stop by and say hello, maybe have a glass of juice and visit before heading for home. As he walked up on to the porch, an unidentified car raced by and a bullet fired from the car struck him in the temple, killing him instantly.

On the last day of school a second grader was walking to a neighboring elementary school to meet his family. They were attending the sixth-grade promotion ceremony for his oldest sister. The ceremony ran late and his mother started walking toward his school to meet him on his designated route. She heard the noise of the truck that hit her son and saw it drive away leaving him dead in the street.

Our schools took on a special role when each of these children died. The staff members were deeply affected by the loss of the students, but they managed to maintain their composure to assist others. In each case they immediately reached out to the families and provided a gathering place for people to meet and grieve together. They provided psychologists and other trained adults to meet one on one and in small groups with whoever needed to talk or just be quiet. They facilitated conversations that were developmentally appropriate for the age of students. In some cases students wrote letters, they planted a tree, or they attended a memorial service. They even arranged to collect money to help pay for funerals. In each case, the adults at the schools were key players in helping others.

No matter how large the school, when a student dies, it is like losing a family member. Even though we may not know the surviving family members well, we know that our actions make a difference for them, the community members and for the other students at the school.

As superintendent, my job is to not only support the family, but to support the staff through their grief. I typically visit the school to symbolically provide support, and I frequently write to the principal and others to express my gratitude for their efforts in helping everyone through a difficult time. While I rarely know the students on a personal level, I still recognized how these tragedies take a toll on all of us who are left to deal with the death of a child.

Tragedy Strikes

Over the past years, we have experienced the deaths of several children. How does anyone cope with such tragedy? How does a superintendent cope with such tragedy? One third grader died in an accidental bathtub drowning, and another died from head trauma after being thrown from his bicycle and hit by a car. A kindergarten child died this year in a family car accident during their vacation. What does one do?

There is no amount of training nor discussion that can ever prepare a school leader for addressing the termination of anyone's life, but it is particularly anguishing and gut-wrenching when you are dealing with the life of a young child. The inevitable "why?" is repeated over and over again with no satisfactory response.

Fortunately, we have established strong team leadership so that the physical and emotional responsibilities are shared. Our principals and assistant superintendent have been instrumental in assisting families in arranging burials and memorials. Specialists provide the most critical emotional support not only to the families involved but also to classmates and staff members.

Although it is one of the most dreadful experiences and one I wish to avoid, the significance of the school district leader's presence at the funeral or memorial service cannot be underestimated. The superintendent represents and conveys the sorrow of the entire school district. The position provides both symbolic and concrete support in the attempt to provide comfort to students, families and staff.

We have learned that it is most helpful to provide time for students to openly discuss and share their feelings if they wish. It has also been helpful to establish a permanent memorial such as an engraved bench or a live tree and/or a garden dedicated at a special ceremony. Addressing students on such occasions can be a challenge, but the message is focused on positive memories.

CoSA

Is it possible to create a school where every student has a place? Where every teacher can develop programs to capture students' interests and fulfill their dreams? Where support staff knows how and why their fine work is essential to creating an excellent school?

First, we have to be honest about who does or doesn't connect now in our current school design—the students, faculty, and staff. Then we must ask ourselves and each other, "What must we do so all people have a place where they can do their best work and achieve their dreams?"

At a high school, we did just that. We had a team of faculty and staff look at all of our students to see how they were connected and, if they weren't, how we might make a connection. Teachers were asked to dream their ultimate dreams in creating programs they thought would appeal to students.

And we asked parents and community about the kinds of programs they thought we needed and what kind they would be willing to support.

One response was a program focused on the arts. A handful of teachers passionately believed they could reach kids through art, music, and drama. Of course, there were those who were skeptical, wondering if this dreaming was just another exercise in futility.

With some leaders, perhaps it might be futile, but not with their principal. This principal was a dreamer *and* a doer. As superintendent, this principal certainly was my dream. He was the principal I always wanted—smart, energetic, entrepreneurial, fun, and persistent. It was easy, and exciting, to offer my support and encouragement.

The result of investigating, planning, questioning, discussing, and redesigning in an iterative process—all the normal steps in setting up a new program—was CoSA, the Collins School of the Arts, a school within a high school.

Naturally we dealt with skeptical and questioning faculty, parents and community members. There were questions about cost, facilities, special treatment and privilege for favored teachers, the wisdom of admitting kids from outside the district, etc.

But it happened! The program started with some very excited and unbelieving kids! The skepticism did not go away, but it diminished, and we were determined to let the results tell the story.

All the students, "our" kids (the students living within our district boundaries) and "their" kids, blurred and became "our" kids. Without question, the proportion of the student body sporting unusual hair colors and wearing jewelry in various body parts increased; so did the evidence of outgoing, exuberant behavior. At any moment, one of the singers or actors walking down the hall might burst into song.

The reality is, this behavior lightened the mood of the campus and brought smiles to lots of faces—both kids and adults. Another byproduct of CoSA was its effect on non-CoSA kids. Students sensed a safer environment, one in which they could express their own diversity more openly.

There were other wonderful outcomes. An amazing array of art adorned hallways and coffee shops in town. Special plays and concerts drew larger-than-ever audiences; community members who attended regional theaters started coming to the high school for evenings of drama and music.

Now some students who "didn't fit" and were alienated had a place. Teachers realized their dreams and developed programs and relationships far beyond what they ever imagined.

CoSA, and several other programs that were developed, came from a commitment to look carefully at our students and to find ways to connect them to the school—to be sure they knew the school belonged to them.

LESSONS LEARNED

- Take a personal interest in students' lives and be rewarded.
- Be the chief advocate for every student's best interest.
- Make community organizations and service clubs partners for students.
- Mine noneducational resources for public schools.
- Share personal stories to motivate students to overcome difficulties.
- Never give up on any student.
- Look to students for inspiration.
- Find student "hero" stories everywhere.
- Understand you often will never know the impact of your work.
- Listen to the wisdom of children.

- Keep gifts from children as treasures and inspiration.
- Ensure fairness for all youngsters.
- Teach children empathy for other children.
- Be bold in creating ways for every student to connect with school.
- Make sure schools are safe places for every student.
- Turn the death of a student into a symbol of inspiration and caring.

Chapter 5

❖

Knowing Yourself

"Now I look back and realize how anxiety-ridden I was. I was all alone and had no one to talk with. It was a true test of my ability to problem solve. I was embarrassed to be seen as a failure. At that time, I thought no one else would understand. Later I found out others had similar experiences."

Assuming responsibility for leading a public school district takes a great deal of inner resolve. During the rough times and the high and low times, you become well acquainted with your personal values and beliefs. You learn what it takes to sustain yourself when you feel that things are out of control. You come face to face with your own inadequacies and learn to reach deep inside yourself for the courage to hang on. You discover that you really were not as well prepared for the role as you thought, and you learn that every single day has the potential to thrust you into the darkest despair or the most extreme exhilaration.

Throughout these challenges you realize that the ups and downs of the profession are what is constant. You learn that you experience the journey alone and that you must get to know yourself very intimately. You must emphasize building relationships since others in the organization are on the ups and downs with you. As superintendent you need to know how interpersonal interactions affect the organization and what it takes to keep the organization on track to meet the purpose of quality teaching and learning. You start by knowing yourself.

PERSONAL QUALITIES THAT COUNT

"Sometimes I have days when I close the door to my office and wonder why anyone hired me to do this job. As a first-time superintendent, I am convinced you're never really prepared for what this job demands or for how to do it. What I have come to understand after a
few years is the importance of trusting your intuition and knowing
your own personal strengths."

Being Calm in the Face of Adversity

Controversy surrounded the district when I arrived. I was not fully
prepared for the attacks on the district from the media as well as from
people inside the system. What I have come to understand is that my
personal calmness and objectivity have helped me, the board, and the
district to come through with most relationships intact. This has been
reinforced many times.

Recently a high school teacher and coach whom I respect greatly
shared with me a reinforcing perspective. I was working on a difficult
situation with a high school staff in the district. I spent an entire day
meeting with staff period by period to answer questions, to listen, and
to give feedback. My teacher-coach colleague shared the next day how
important my serenity, as he calls it, helped both to address the situation honestly and to provide some reinforcement to the staff.

Superintendents often face tense situations that threaten their survival. They soon learn tough challenges become the norm and it is essential to learn to face challenges with calmness, serenity, and on occasion even laughter. With all of the turmoil this job demands, I have felt
many times the importance of staying outwardly calm. While inside I
may be churning, I know that others need to sense my calmness.

Collegial Kindness: Giving and Gaining Courage

"From those first kind words from a colleague, I have had an internal sense of just how okay it is to feel vulnerable."

It was my first principalship; I felt so confident and upbeat. I had finished my doctorate and had some teaching experiences, and I was
ready to lead the best school in the state at the age of twenty-nine. How
fleeting was that feeling. A few days into my new position, I received

the agenda for the first district management team meeting. I was instantly nervous. I walked into the conference room, and although I recognized a couple of the individuals that had interviewed me, every other face was unfamiliar. At that moment, one person, through one simple act, gave me the courage I needed. Bob, the high school principal (and the most senior administrator) must have sensed my anxiety. He leaned close to me and in the gentlest way said, "You may not understand a lot of what's said today, but don't worry. I'll help you out." As the meeting progressed and the unknowns starting stacking up, I smiled inside as I discovered how little I really did know about administration. I may have looked confident, but inside was mild panic and my new colleague knew that. Interspersed with the panic was the reassurance of those kind words and an even kinder, experienced face across the table. I knew I had a friend for life.

A few weeks later when I received the first multi-paged printout of my school site budget, I was once again faced with anxiety. I retreated to the privacy of my office so no one would sense my lack of understanding of the "hieroglyphics" before me. The knot in my stomach tightened as I thought that I should understand all this. The anxiety subsided with the knowledge that Bob would guide me through this too.

From those first kind words from a colleague, I have had an internal sense of just how okay it is to feel vulnerable. That simple first gesture provided for me the foundation of courage that I have carried throughout my administrative career. For many years, I have passed on the same gentle words of support to other administrators facing new positions.

Listening and Listening Well!

Good leaders are often very good talkers, and they like to talk. Leaders often have developed highly refined speaking skills and presentation abilities. Good talkers grab our attention and they motivate us. As leaders, we all work hard at developing these skills. We talk to inspire others. We demonstrate our abilities and our capabilities in leading an organization forward by strong verbal presentations to our teams.

However, we need to continually remind ourselves that listening is almost always as influential, persuasive and confidence building as talking. If we want to be effective as leaders, we must first listen. As

Stephen Covey states in his book *Seven Habits of Highly Effective Behavior*, "We must seek first to understand, and then be understood."

Good leaders listen. Great leaders sit at the edge of their chairs and really listen. Really great leaders listen intently. If there is one thing I have learned in my twenty-seven years in education, it is to quit talking and start listening. Many years ago I heard a simple adage: There is a very real reason why people are born with two ears and only one mouth. They're born with two ears for listening and only one mouth for talking.

With a solitary focus on listening and listening well, we acknowledge others. When we acknowledge through listening, we are demonstrating effective leadership behavior. At its foundation is the core belief that what others express and feel is more important than what the leader has to say. You cannot set direction for a successful organization without listening to others.

Being Ethical

> "In small towns, rumors often dominate the communications system. I have always found this difficult to deal with, especially when the rumors seem to be mean-spirited."

A couple of years ago, I was faced with a situation when a principal had come under attack from some parents. The onslaught began with the resignation of a popular staff member in the school. He had resigned because of some questionable financial transactions involving school funds. The resignation seemed to be the final straw as it related to the principal and his relationship with the parents. The parents were certain that the principal set the man up to lose his job and that the inappropriate financial actions really never occurred. The only thing that seemed likely to appease the parents was for the principal to also lose his job.

While the principal had clearly created some problems at the school, he was not responsible for what happened to the teacher. My ethical dilemma was how to maintain the confidentiality of the employee who had resigned pending a full audit and how to provide some protection or defense for the principal.

I could have used the rumor mill to drop hints about what the staff member had done with the money, or I could have attempted to address the problems of the principal in a more logical way. I also wanted to convey a message that a group of parents could not simply band together to force the principal's removal without due process.

Ultimately we hired an outside consultant to assess the situation, determine the status of staff and principal relationships, and make recommendations. Parents wanted the assessment report to be made public, but we could not release the information because of the protected confidential nature of the information.

The principal accepted a position outside the district. Even with that, the parents still wanted to bring back the teacher. The audit revealed even more irregularities than we had known prior to the resignation, but we maintained confidentiality. While it could have helped to go public to dispel the idea that we had forced the resignation and to dispel the parent's assumption that there had been no misuse of funds, we chose to be professional and private about all the information we had.

SOURCES OF GUIDANCE AND INSPIRATION

"Over a period of years, I've learned some simple yet powerful lessons that have provided me strength for addressing tough issues. When I need encouragement, I draw on these experiences, which allow me to move successfully ahead. These simple lessons have pulled me through many challenging situations."

My Personal Board of Directors: Relationships Built for a Lifetime

Whenever I face a challenge without a clear path to follow, I focus on individuals I've admired. I find myself speculating on how they might address the latest challenge. As I began my administrative career, I was encouraged to describe the qualities of the significant individuals who have guided me throughout life. This collection of individuals I rely on is my personal "board of directors." This board of directors has proved to be one of the most effective tools for me to remind myself and those with whom I work about the power of relationships.

It's very simple. Here's how it works. Take any piece of paper and draw an oval. Think about the role of a board of directors. A board advises, evaluates, provides feedback, presents ideas, helps in reflection and serves as a guiding force. There are many forms of boards of directors. There are church councils, PTA boards, soccer leagues, and school boards. There are corporate boards and city councils. These advisory groups are everywhere in our lives.

In looking at the blank paper with the penciled oval, think of this as your own personal board of directors. Around the table list the names of those people who have been central influences in your life. Take quiet moments to think about these individuals. There are parents and friends, colleagues and children. For me, my board has always included two high school musical theater teachers who made small town kids feel like Broadway stars. When all the names are recorded around that oval table on the paper, take time to reflect on personal characteristics displayed by those people. Characteristics often listed are: sense of humor, caring attitude, honesty, integrity and fairness. Mentioned often are individuals who have loved unconditionally, who were thoughtful, attentive, and warm, and who had the ability to instill a sense of self-worth. Most significantly, almost everyone's list includes individuals who are good listeners.

As a superintendent, I continue to use the board of directors exercise; through this exercise, I am strengthened professionally. Through the recall of the significant individuals in my life, I am able to regain personal strength. I'm able to become a better learner and better teacher by displaying the characteristics I value the most. I'm able to reflect on the power of building, nourishing, and maintaining relationships. It reminds me what I need to do to exhibit the characteristics I have valued in my relationships. This revisiting of my "board of directors" becomes a respite period in the harried days of the superintendency. It allows me to think fundamentally about who I am, where I came from, and who is important to me. I am reminded that I need to display those same characteristics that have been significant for me so I can become the kind of leader who takes a place on others' "boards of directors."

Treasure Your Past to Inspire Your Future

> "Reading a letter from a struggling student who finally made it or a note from a colleague with whom you've worked can provide a touch of reassurance that you may need."

I'm a saver. I have crumbled, yellowed news clippings, magazine articles with frayed edges, and notes on napkins. I have saved outlines from every speech I've given and countless notes from speeches I've heard. I have lists of funny things kids have said in classrooms and copies of student work that have struck me as humorous or heart wrenching. I have notes from parents expressing thanks and journal entries that I've made when I've had some profound learning experiences. A recent addition to my collection is a colorful Volvo advertisement encouraging prospective buyers to "Find Your Own Road!"

I have this treasured collection in a nearly full file cabinet. Poetry written by my mother, business cards from past positions along with countless mementos of my career have been gathered in a special spot in my office. When I work with teachers or beginning administrators, I encourage them to start saving little treasures that have inspired or touched them. I often tell them that one day they'll need to rely on them to bring back self-confidence, courage and a positive approach during difficult times. Education is synonymous with tough challenges, and I've reminded them that they'll need ready access to inspirational mementos. Reading a letter from a struggling student who finally made it or a note from a colleague with whom you've worked can provide the touch of reassurance that we all need.

Call a Colleague

"A mentor of mine told me that the superintendency is a very lonely job—he was right in many ways."

What I have discovered is that my professional development often comes from other superintendents. Situations arise. I am unable to find a book or journal to help; my coursework in the doctoral program didn't focus on the problem at hand. I call a colleague.

Early in my first superintendency, I was dealing with a principal who tended not to communicate with the district staff, and I was surprised one too many times. I spoke with him about my concerns. His response was to turn to a board member. Fortunately, the board member told him that it was inappropriate to come to him as a board member. He suggested that the principal come to me and then indicated that he would let me know of the principal's communication.

My initial reaction was anger and disappointment. When I became more rational, I called a long-time mentor to ask advice. In brainstorming ways to best address the problem and still keep a principal feeling successful, I gained valuable professional development.

I continue to attend workshops and read professional literature, but it is so often other superintendent colleagues who provide the best training. A mentor of mine told me that the superintendency is a very lonely job—he was right in many ways. But I know that loneliness ends with a phone call to another respected superintendent.

PROFESSIONAL DEVELOPMENT NEVER ENDS

"Professional development, whether workshops or a doctoral program, has always been important to me. While I felt prepared for the superintendency, I have been reminded of the absolute need to continue my training. Recently, one of my newer board members said, 'I keep finding new things I don't know about this board role.' So it goes for the superintendency."

The Dilemma of Taking Time for Development

Along with knowing what your core values and beliefs are and the knowledge of self that comes from life experience, every superintendent needs to make a commitment to be a continuous learner. It is critical to stay abreast of the knowledge and skills required to lead a dynamic school district.

In my first year as a superintendent, I discovered that each day's mail brought notices and invitations to attend conferences, workshops, meetings, seminars, institutes, and even college and university courses. They addressed all sorts of topics related to the superintendency as well as current issues that swirled across my desk. I called the search consultant who had placed me in the job to discuss the dilemma of making the right professional development choices. He advised, "During the first year or two, you need to go to as many opportunities for training as you can and then decide which ones are most valuable and return to those during the following years." I got a similar response when I asked other practicing superintendents for their opinions. Usually each one would recommend a favorite based on a topic or issue that was most relevant to them at that point in time. There seemed to be little consensus.

After my first year, I realized that determining which professional development opportunities to attend was far more complex than I had anticipated. Making choices about what to attend involved more than just selecting a topic or an issue. It also involved such choices as thinking about which groups of people or organizations would be able to give me the most valuable perspective. I needed to consider how far I wanted to travel and how much time I had. I need to know if I was looking for a regional, state or national point of view. I also had to decide if there were others in the organization that I should take with me such as board members, staff, students, parents or community members who could help me disseminate the information that was presented.

As I sorted through the many choices, I also learned to consider who else would be attending the event. Would I have an opportunity to meet others outside of public education and discuss common concerns? Was I looking for a group of superintendents to share their point of view on a particular topic? Did I want to hear from a mixed group of public school employees rather than only my peer group?

One summer I went to a wonderful science curriculum workshop organized by and for teachers; it was invaluable to me in learning about the new science framework. At first, everyone was concerned that I was the only superintendent in attendance, but they soon recognized my genuine interest and allowed me to become one of the group.

After I attended my first annual California Superintendents' Symposium, I knew that I would attend every year as long as I was a superintendent. Interesting, diverse workshops were conducted, and speakers presented relevant topics to rooms full of superintendents who then discussed the implications for the state and their individual districts. I always came home with valuable ideas and information.

Each time I attend a workshop or conference, I consider its value to me and the district and determine whether I will attend again or recommend it to others. Sometimes I regret my decision to attend certain events, but I know that even when I have made a bad choice about how to best use my time, it is always a learning experience. Continuous learning and professional development are critical to my success as a leader, and I need to keep addressing which opportunities will be of most value to me and the organization.

What Happens When You're Gone

I recognize how important it is to stay current in my job, and I usually plan to attend several professional development opportunities throughout the school year. I also understand the importance of keeping my job balanced with my personal life. I plan annual vacations so I can get away from the day-to-day demands of the position. The challenge I face when I leave the district, whether it is for professional or personal reasons, is "What will happen when I am gone?"

It is almost comical to watch superintendents at professional development conferences during break time. We rush to pay phones or pull out our cell phones and call the office just to "check in and see how things are going." Even when we have very competent people at home who can address whatever needs arise, we still feel compelled to let everyone know we are thinking about them. We even send faxes back and forth, check our voice mail, our e-mail, and we make every effort to keep up with daily operations.

When I accepted my first superintendency, I told Joe, a friend who was a long-time superintendent, that I was planning to take a two-week vacation to the Midwest before I formally started my new position. He responded that he wished me a great vacation and emphasized that I should enjoy it thoroughly, because it would be the last time I would go away and not worry about what was happening in the district. I remember laughing and saying that would never apply to me. Well, I discovered he was absolutely correct. I soon learned that if something happens in the district when I am gone, I should have been there to handle it. It doesn't mean that there is no one there who can take care of problem. I have worked hard to make sure there are capable people in the district to handle situations when I am away. It simply means that the board members, staff, and community members expect the superintendent to be the person at the helm at all times and there is no one who can substitute in a crisis.

On vacations, in spite of everyone admonishing me to not worry about a thing, I still call in periodically to "check in and see how things are going."

Learning to Laugh with Colleagues

> "Professional development can be done in many ways. Sometimes the simplest are overlooked."

Our Coco's Restaurant group developed out of the need of two brand new, shell-shocked superintendents to find the answer to the question "What's my job?"

In our excited yet bewildered state as new appointees, a colleague and I asked two experienced superintendents to join us for breakfast to share their advice and wisdom with us. Fortunately, they did. In fact, they were delighted to help. With graciousness and charm, these veterans coached, cajoled, suggested, and reassured us as we muddled through those first few months.

Frankly, the two of us rookies were awed when our mentors talked about instructional initiatives they were promoting in their districts. As we confessed our attempts to satisfy some low-level, Maslow-type needs in our districts, they assured us that we, too, would soon be talking about learning and teaching. Their advice and suggestions helped us with specifics, but their extraordinary gift to us was their reassurance about our ability to progress and guide our districts.

After several breakfast meetings, the Coco's group was established, and it continues as an institution. When the original two veterans left, we beginners kept the breakfasts going, with invitations to new colleagues.

Our Coco's group is now in its tenth year and is guided by a very loose, but important set of rules:

1. We set the next meeting before we leave each breakfast and find a date that suits most.
2. A memo is sent to all as a reminder of the next meeting and informing those who missed.
3. There are no agendas, no minutes, and no follow-up "to do" lists, other than a follow-up request of an individual for some assistance.
4. No one can dominate or hold court. If anyone does, he or she is spoken to quietly and individually and then left off the meeting list.
5. Sometimes people will agree to bring a work sample to share so everyone can get a new idea. For example, at one meeting every superintendent brought their board agenda and described why it was done as it was. We shared the process for preparing the agenda and running the meeting and shared perspectives on what worked and what did not.
6. When anyone's been in the newspaper, he or she is teased (gently and warmly) and thanked for helping to keep the others off the front page, at least for one day.
7. When a superintendent or a district experiences success, we all celebrate.
8. Ideas, thoughts, and dreams are shared with friendly critics present to respond.

The point of these meetings is made clear to all—fellowship, sharing, and laughter. Relationships are built so people have others to turn to for advice, solace, and joy.

We all leave each breakfast, if not laughing, at least smiling and feeling rejuvenated. Those who took the time to squeeze Coco's in despite the huge demands are always grateful.

Ensuring that you grow as a superintendent requires you to look at various aspects of professional development. Not only do you need traditional, professional development that focuses on learning the content and processes of the requisite skills needed for superintending, but you also need to make time to have informal meetings with other superintendents regularly for fellowship and support. Both contribute to the continuous learning that is integral to success in the ever changing and challenging role of superintendent.

SURVIVING AND THRIVING

"I learned the significance of short-term pain for long-term goals."

Being a Good Target

In my first year as superintendent, principals stated that the seniority-driven teacher transfer process eliminated their ability to select appropriate staff to enhance programs for students. This process also provided an escape mechanism for marginal teachers to move whenever they felt the pressure of teaching accountability. This was a serious issue, but the teachers' association perceived seniority rights as a basic human right, and any attempt to change the process was received as a declaration of war.

The school board was united in its determination to restore the responsibility of staff selection to be based on a variety of criteria and not only seniority. Ironically, the collective bargaining contract did not restrict transfer selection to seniority; however, the practice was historically followed. A protracted, hostile bargaining session resulted in public rallies, negative publications, and media coverage regarding my leadership. There were cries for a strike and a "vote of no confidence" in the superintendent and the board. There was continuous vilification of me through a variety of tactics.

It was a shocking turn of events during the initial honeymoon phase. I was not prepared for the anger and personal attacks. What does this mean? Is my credibility destroyed? Can I still be an effective leader? Why is this happening? I experienced feelings of isolation and loneliness. My emotions included denial, hurt, self-doubt, fear of failure, and anger. It was a major struggle to separate personal emotions from the professional responsibility to represent the school district in a positive, dignified manner.

When I made inquiries with the union leadership, they pointed out that being a target comes with the territory. They were adamant that they were not attacking me personally but only my role. It was a long time before I was able to accept that point of view. I had discovered a document from a teachers' association listing strategies to control bargaining such as: attack the superintendent for "his" autocratic leadership style and deliberately misinform members to create dissatisfaction with the district.

During this period, the administrators' association leadership approached me with a proposal to present a "vote of confidence" public message to counter the negative publicity created by the union. It was a tempting offer which made me feel better but I questioned the impact. The process would enhance my own self-confidence, but it would create divisions between principals, teachers and parents. The potential for creating separate camps of pros and cons would not contribute to a unity of purpose and focus on the whole. It would make no sense for the principals to also become targets. I informed the administrators' association leadership that I appreciated their support. There was no need to demonstrate in a public manner. I learned the significance of short-term pain for long-term gains. I understood that confronting the seniority issue was the foundation for challenging the status quo and ultimately redesigning a new structure for decision making.

Although the union used many wedge strategies, the board and I did not falter in our unity. In fact, the greater the pressure tactics, the stronger team unity became.

Caught in the Middle and Working to Take Control

"As I came to work one day, I found myself face to face with a demonstration in front of one of my high schools."

Several years ago, I reviewed the California middle school report titled "Caught in the Middle." This document describes the special needs of adolescents in the middle grades. It proposes several solutions for improving their schooling. As I reflect on my work as a superintendent in today's openly hostile environment toward public education in California, I find myself literally "caught in the middle." I am caught between the powerful money interest groups who sponsor legislation through the initiative process and special interest groups seeking power through the use of the state and federal complaint processes. Both groups cause local districts to spend an inordinate share of their resources on matters that bear little relationship to the teaching and learning process, or on building positive relationships in the community.

Early in my superintendency, a challenging piece of new state legislation triggered major local demonstrations. As I came to work one day, I found myself face to face with 250 demonstrators and print and television media in front of one of my high schools. I discovered that a disgruntled former employee had convinced a small group to distribute flyers listing me among a group of district individuals who should be fired. During the day of the original large demonstration, and for several days following, I had to deal with the needs and concerns of every stakeholder in the district and some outside of our boundaries. My days were spent with law enforcement, attorneys, the board, parents, administrators, teachers, influential community members, and students. As I communicated with each group, I tried to determine their needs. My solution was to list each stakeholder and tailor my communication to those identified needs.

Although survival was my initial concern, this situation prepared me for the challenges to come. I now face each new challenge calmly because I know that I can respond to our detractors and support our students and teachers by tailoring my communications to recognize the needs of the various stakeholder groups.

Having a Vision Means You're Never Unprepared

"Here I was about to embark on my first superintendency and I had no time to prepare my debut remarks."

A few days after the board of trustees formally approved my first contract as superintendent, I was invited to attend the annual staff recognition banquet held at the high school. I decided to make the one-and-a-half-hour trip early so that I could spend some time in the district getting to know people at the central office. When I arrived in the early afternoon, the superintendent's secretary informed me that the acting superintendent had gone home ill and there was no one to take his place as emcee for this important event.

You guessed it—I was expected to step in and take over! Once that decision was determined, we all started to work on the last-minute details. I asked a veteran secretary to sit down with me to help me practice pronouncing correctly the names of all the people to be recognized. Engraved plaques and pens were to be handed out for years of service and other significant accomplishments. All board members were to be there, as were many other community leaders.

I had a few minutes to visit with other staff before I loaded all of the awards in my car and went to the school early to see how I could help. I put centerpieces on tables, set up chairs, and put plastic liners in the trashcans. As people arrived, it dawned on me that I would be expected to give some kind of a speech at my first appearance in the district.

Many years ago I acknowledged a gap in my skills as a leader. I discovered that to be able to give a decent speech, I needed to prepare. I could not just stand up and be a scintillating orator. Here I was about to embark on my first superintendency and I had no time to prepare my debut remarks.

I decided that the safest topic for me to speak on was my thoughts about my role and vision as superintendent. That would give everyone a chance to get to know me a little bit and to understand how I viewed this new opportunity.

After a quick introduction about my family and formal schooling, I began by telling the group that I believed there are two kinds of people who work in a public school district—teachers and support people. I am a support person and I work along with all other support people to ensure that teachers and students have optimal conditions for teaching and learning. I went on to tell them that I would do everything that I could to ensure that no matter what challenges confronted us, we would all stay focused on the purpose of our organization—quality teaching and learning. I shared my four or five big goals for the year and asked for their support and encouragement as I moved to the community and set out to learn how to be effective as their superintendent. I may have made a few other comments, but I have no written record of that speech.

The evening went by in a flash, and in spite of my rehearsal, I still stumbled on a few unusual names. The applause was warm, and the atmosphere was festive. As I made that long drive home, I was certainly happy that I had reflected many times about the dimensions of my role as superintendent. It enabled me to stand up and give a very important impromptu speech.

KNOWING WHEN IT'S TIME TO LEAVE

"I have often heard administrators say that when it's not fun anymore they will leave. Being a superintendent is rarely fun. It is a challenging, satisfying, rewarding, confounding, and incomparable experience, but rarely fun."

During a particularly stormy session with a group of contentious faculty members, one of our secondary principals commented to the staff, "our students are not throw-away children, and we will treat them as though they all have the potential to learn; if you don't believe that, some of you in this room need to rethink, relocate, or retire." This was a shot heard 'round the district. The principal later apologized for his harsh words. Many faculty members privately rejoiced in his finally letting a few of his colleagues, who resisted changing demographics, know their available choices.

The principal's words to his faculty to rethink, relocate or retire brought to my consciousness the choices that were available to me at various points in my career as a superintendent. At the time of this writing, I have served as a superintendent in a suburban/rural community for six years and spent a total of thirty-one years in public education. I was appointed from inside the district and enjoyed a favorable relationship with all five board members in my former position as an assistant superintendent. For the first six months, everything seemed to be fine. About six months into my tenure as superintendent, two board members became increasingly demanding and consistently requested the dismissal of two of our high school principals. One complained about everything I did and began a campaign to undermine me. They were correct in their assessment of the two principals; but this clearly was not within their purview as individual board members.

At that point in my career, the only option available to me was to re-think my approach to my job. I made certain that the entire board was kept informed of any request for information by any board members. Fortunately, the other board members saw through their requests and would have no part of their strategy. As I went home each evening thinking about how miserable I felt, I thought about the options available to me. I could not relocate. What board would hire a superintendent who had spent only six months in her present assignment? At that time, retirement was not an option.

A board election during my third year gave the board majority to my tormentors. I gave serious thought to relocating, because by this time, it seemed that I had encountered it all, including the highs and lows of any superintendency. I had experienced 250 demonstrators in front of a high school. I had witnessed police in riot gear in response to a student suspension. Wildfires had threatened our schools, causing evacuations. I dealt with shoddy contractors, resulting in lawsuits, and attempts had been made to recall two board members. The eighteen-year-old girlfriend of a fired teacher was elected to the school board, and a demoted administrator staged a hunger strike and planned a sick-out.

On the positive side, I had experienced unprecedented support by the site level PTAs, service clubs, and the chief negotiator for the teachers' union. Classified employees' relations could not have been better. We developed a strategic plan and a facilities master plan, we changed boundaries twice with few public complaints, and we implemented every reform dictated by the legislature. After three years, I felt if I so desired, relocating was an option. In the back of my mind, I always kept a list of my supporters. If I decided to relocate, I could look forward to favorable letters of recommendation from my board officers. Watching other superintendents struggle to relocate, I was fully aware that the record I established in this district would determine, to a great extent, another school board's willingness to employ me. My research showed that boards are interested in a superintendent's relationship with his or her current board, parents, union leaders, community leaders and the principals. I decided not to relocate because I was not mentally or physically prepared to begin the process of developing new relationships in a new place.

A recent board election with three vacant seats again made me think very seriously about retirement. While none of the candidates openly criticized me, not one was very warm to my overtures to provide information about the district. Although invited, none accepted my invitation for a meeting. I knew that two of the current members were just waiting for an opportunity to form a new board majority that would not support me as superintendent. I made a conscious decision that if the three incumbents were not returned to office, I would retire two months later. Fortunately, none of the negative board challengers succeeded in being elected. Therefore, I made the decision to stay in my current position and continue to make a difference for the students in our district.

I have often heard administrators say that when it's not fun anymore they will leave. Being a superintendent is rarely fun. It is a challenging, satisfying, rewarding, confounding, and incomparable experience, but rarely fun. My experience has taught me that your age, length of service in a particular district, board and community support and reasonable success in leading the district are important considerations when a superintendent decides either to rethink her approach to the job, relocate, or retire.

GAINING AND KEEPING PERSPECTIVE

"The challenge is in seeing the whole picture. . . . Sometimes there are clues and pieces of information that come together just as we match colors and shapes in jigsaw pieces."

The Jigsaw Puzzle: The Pieces Eventually Fit

When the death of a friend blind-sided me, a colleague told me, "Life is like a jigsaw puzzle." We both reflected on why this life was ended so suddenly and so senselessly. During our visit, she asked me if I ever did puzzles. A childhood recollection of Mrs. Prince flashed before my eyes. This elderly friend of my mother always had a puzzle in progress on her rickety card table. She always started with the border and the other pieces were spread randomly outside it. I told my friend that every time we visited Mrs. Prince, I'd try to get a few more pieces to fit. "Most people start a jigsaw puzzle by doing the border first," my friend commented. "It's as if they seem to need some sort of organizational structure." We continued to speculate that sometimes life's events are like jigsaw puzzles.

I've thought of this analogy many times in my professional career. Often the parameters of a problem are defined, but the challenge is in seeing the whole picture. Pieces of problems are everywhere and nothing seems to fit. Sometimes there are clues and pieces of information that seem to come together, just as we match colors and shapes in jigsaw pieces. More often, however, there seems to be no real information or clues to rely upon in putting the puzzle together. You need to develop more insight, complete more research or study issues more closely and in different ways. One needs to simply sit, look closely, take time, rearrange, readjust, step away, step forward, and the pieces will eventually fit together.

This simple jigsaw puzzle reminder has provided me many peaceful moments in the face of crisis. When things have been confusing or when I simply haven't known what step to take next, I've stepped back and said to myself quietly, "Here's another piece of the puzzle. Where does this fit?" It's a reminder that it's impossible to know everything...and more importantly, it's okay. It'll all fit together in time.

The Heart Monitor: Ups and Downs Are Normal

"Look at change as the norm. . . . The constant ups and downs of our profession are normal."

Several years ago, when my father was facing his last days in an intensive care unit, I was asked by my siblings to gather details on what would happen as my father slipped away. None of us actually knew the outward physical behaviors that would occur as he neared death. A caring physician described the process of gently slipping away through controlled medication. In his explanation, he pointed toward the heart monitor above Dad's bed. Similar to a television screen, the monitor displayed up and down lines of activity on the screen. "As a loved one weakens, the up and down lines occur in longer intervals and the height of the upward 'blips' lower on the screen. Near death, the line will become flat and the monitor is turned off." With this explanation, the five of us felt comforted and prepared. A short time later, we watched the screen as our father peacefully slipped away. It was a poignant image that I knew I would never forget.

Weeks later, I attended a national education conference. I was right up front when the keynote speaker addressed the hundreds of administrators facing the challenges of public education. In describing the relentless pace we keep to stay current, she encouraged us not to be discouraged but to be motivated by the changes we see for our youth. Along with my colleagues in attendance, I was stirred by her speech and I was ready to return to my district on Monday morning with new enthusiasm. "Look at change as the norm," she emphasized. "The constant ups and downs of our profession are normal." And then, as if she were speaking directly to me (and I'm certain she was), she asked us to visualize a heart monitor next to a dying patient in intensive care. "As a patient dies," she described, "the line on the screen gradually becomes flat." "When you have constant ups and downs, you should feel joyous because you are alive!" I was temporarily immobilized, with tears tumbling down my cheeks. From that day, I have shared this heart monitor analogy. As I reach out to encourage my colleagues, I often use the heart monitor as a fitting visual image of experiencing life's ups and downs. I coach teachers, principals, and parents to accept criticism, challenges, and questions as signs of a healthy organization.

TAKING CARE OF YOURSELF

Balancing Self, Spouse, and Family

> "During my first year as a superintendent, I rarely exercised, began to gain weight, and hated the way I felt physically. I had to do something."

The word "balance" may be overused and seemingly impossible to achieve in this fast-paced world in which we live. My father died at the young age of fifty, my current age. I painfully realized at that time that life is often too short and that we should be enjoying every day.

I love my job, I enjoy its many challenges, and I respect the many wonderful educators with whom I work. However, I made it clear early on with my board that my job would not be my life. My husband, family, and friends are very important to me, and the job is not worth damaging those relationships.

Sometimes it takes little things to help provide some balance to the many hours and demands of the job. I have a few habits that assist me in getting off the roller coaster. I love crossword puzzles and make sure I take time nearly every day to work the *Los Angeles Times* puzzle. It is an escape, gives me new vocabulary and puts me in the world of words that I enjoy. I keep a novel going at all times—usually the mystery, detective, or "trash" kind. Everyone needs a little escape, and books do that for me.

During my first year as a superintendent, I rarely exercised, began to gain weight, and hated the way I felt physically. I had to do something. I walked at least three or four times a week. I even allowed myself one or two of the days to be weekdays—meaning I arrived at work by 8 a.m. instead of 7 a.m. The office is still standing, and I feel better. Walking means having great conversations with myself and taking time to enjoy fresh air.

My husband and I have a tradition on Sunday mornings. We read the Sunday paper in our living room, listen to classical music, and drink tea. It's a quiet time and one that is very special to us. Mom lives close, and I make sure to talk to her nearly every day and see her every week, as we do with our best friends. Each of these tiny pieces of time and treasured activities helps me keep things in perspective and keep me fresh for the job.

Enhancing Your Environment

"Where do you do your best thinking? In the bathtub, in the shower, walking the neighborhood with your headphones, or sitting in the kitchen in the middle of the night? Do you think best in the library or early in the morning, on a park bench or at your desk?"

Wherever you do your best thinking, fill your environment with the motivational tools you need to create and problem solve. I glanced around my office as I struggled with a solution to a challenge I faced. I reflected on all the important things I have placed in my office and why I have them there. My environment is my inspiration. Since then, I've added even a few more touches to further surround myself with little touches of inspiration.

I have a set of children's books that I received from my mother when I was 11 years old. On that golden birthday, she gave me 11 books on August 11! I read them all many times as a child, and I remember those good feelings of familiarity as I flip through the pages. Tucked in another corner is an old brick painted like a schoolhouse that I picked up on a vacation in Door County, Wisconsin, the site of many family vacations. On an open wall is a huge self-portrait of my twenty-three-year old daughter just as she discovered water colors in the first grade.

A quilt mounted on another wall was stitched lovingly by a school librarian when I left the elementary school principalship to take a new position. I read to every classroom every month in that school and the children had drawn favorite characters on fabric now collected in a quilted treasure. I can remember every child whose name is recorded on the bottom of each square.

A print called *Heart and Soul* hangs above my desk. A gift from two college roommates, it is framed in a purple, pink and royal blue study of hearts and circles, and was done by a struggling, college artist friend. Its passion and profound message have touched many lives. Her commitment to her craft has placed her now as one of the Midwest's leading printmakers with a legendary following.

If you want to be creative and innovative, create a setting and environment that will inspire you.

The business manager with whom I worked for many years had fresh flowers delivered to her office every Monday morning. Never knowing exactly what combination would arrive each week, she was inspired by the surprise and the beauty in nature. She often told me that when she felt harried, she'd simply look closely at every flower and appreciate life in its simplest form. It gave her the few minutes of respite she needed to get back on track.

Spaces are powerful. Significant research has been done on environments. There is no doubt that chrome, glass, black marble, and white walls make a statement. Modernistic chairs without arms give a message of austerity, slickness, efficiency, and no nonsense. Conversely, upholstered chairs with wooden arms and plush sofas in warm, earthy tones give a different message entirely.

I have a friend who owns a company that designs the interiors of large carriers, ocean vessels and navy cruisers. He designs them with a high degree of knowledge about the impact of color in the environment. The cramped cafeterias are red, yellow, and orange—hot colors that say "get in, eat quickly, and get out." Because of limited space, those vessels need to be designed with food lines that move quickly. The bunking areas are blues, greens, and gentle beiges that establish an atmosphere of relaxation, restfulness, and silence.

A teacher friend in Laguna Beach creates an Asian aura with her third-grade students when she fills her room with porcelain lamps covered with Chinese and Japanese symbols. The mats, wicker placements, and large blue floor pillows create an ambiance. Silk and cotton fabrics are draped over chairs, and tables hold solitary flower stems in simple vases. The lights are dimmed and the student poets are inspired to write beautiful, thoughtful passages.

Our environments are also ourselves. Add a scarf, add a pin, wear striped socks and colorful Keds. When it comes to sustaining ourselves we must look at ourselves and find clothing, sweaters, and fabrics that inspire.

With these crazy lives we lead and with increasing demands on our time, we have few moments of quiet and we need inspired surroundings. Take a look around. If your "best thinking spaces" need a lift, take the time to add a few touches of inspiration.

Take care of yourself as you create an environment that contributes to the quality of your work. Your surroundings can help sustain you during difficult moments and even inspire you.

FINAL STORY

A new and important "Knowing Yourself" story emerged out of these meetings of eight women superintendents. Our reasons for agreeing to this book writing effort varied, but we were drawn together out of the commonality of experiences, and our never-ending curiosity for new and interesting projects.

Part of the attraction was the opportunity to get to know superintendents, some of whom we knew as professional colleagues at meetings and conferences. Some of us, however, were only names to each other.

From the first dinner together at a private home, to the weekends squeezed around incredibly busy schedules, to an hour or so snatched preciously away from a conference or meeting, or early Saturday morning at someone's district office, we talked, laughed, and wrote, and rewrote—and got to know and appreciate one another, our similarities and our separate challenges.

Despite the scheduling difficulties, we stayed together, in varying degrees, for some of the same reasons women have over the centuries—to understand themselves, their work, to share and to nurture and improve the lives of others for whom they feel a responsibility. Like women everywhere, we had altruistic notions about what we could and should contribute to the growth of others. But like many efforts that start with looking outward, we inevitably looked inward as well. To a person, we learned an enormous amount about ourselves as well as each other. Though we did the tasks of writing, the power of our efforts came from stopping our normal hectic pace and taking the time to reflect.

Max Landberg says, in his *Tao of Coaching*, "A person cannot see his or her own image in running water but sees it in water that is at rest." How true this was for us who were used to moving at warp speed sixty to eighty hours per week. For a change, we stopped. And out of that stopping, we found another way to bring to life our advice of this last chapter, "Knowing Yourself."

This process of coming together, sharing, laughing, and writing our stories reinforced the importance of each topic of our final chapter: personal qualities that count, sources of guidance and inspiration, professional development never ends, surviving and thriving, gaining and keeping perspective, and taking care of yourself.

Throughout our careers, we had mentors who influenced us in life-changing ways. Now we are mentoring each other. Now we are serving as a source of inspiration for each other. We marvel at the strong qualities and we share in the painful personal events in each others' lives. During our years of writing, one of us went through, and thankfully survived, a brain tumor. Another was successfully treated for breast cancer. Three of us left the superintendency—one for retirement, and two for new careers. One continues to serve in her current district, five moved to new districts. But, regardless of the career moves, the conversations provided a powerful, on-going, and under-appreciated form of professional development. Actually, these conversations do more than assist us in our professional growth, they help us gain and keep our perspective on work, family, and other important aspects of a full life. We started knowing little about each other, and ended knowing the details and dreams of each others' lives, developing bonds far beyond anything we anticipated. Not only did we help each other survive but we helped each other thrive, and we are forever grateful.

LESSONS LEARNED

- Trust your intuition.
- Know your personal strengths.
- Maintain confidentiality—always.

- Remember individuals you have admired.
- Become the kind of leader that others can admire.
- Anticipate change as a norm.
- Reflect for the future.
- Separate personal emotions from professional responsibility.
- Challenge the status quo.
- Face challenges with calmness and, on occasion, even laughter.
- Have a vision that can be articulated at any time.
- Tailor your communication to address the needs of the audience.
- Develop expertise as a politician, manager, and leader.
- Understand the impact of your words and actions.
- Listen.
- Anticipate and prepare for leaving if you feel it's time to go.
- Understand and use your power wisely.
- Learn about the power of an organization.
- Keep your life in balance.
- Maintain a healthy personal life.
- Provide yourself with professional development.
- Keep in touch with other superintendents.
- Your environment could reflect who you are.
- Make certain those left behind know how to reach you when away from the office.

Index

About the Authors

GLORIA L. JOHNSTON

Gloria Johnston is Superintendent of Schools in the West Contra Costa Unified School District, an urban district located in northern California. Nearly 34,000 students are enrolled in preschool through twelfth grade. Prior to this position, she was superintendent in the Banning Unified School District in Riverside County, California.

While working for school districts in California and Illinois, Gloria has been a district-level administrator in the areas of bilingual education, curriculum development, student assessment, state and federal categorical programs, preschool services, and human relations. She also worked as a teacher and principal in schools in Illinois and spent three years teaching English as a second language in Caracas, Venezuela.

Her consulting work has included school districs and state departments of education across the U.S. She has taught college classes in Illinois and California and her most recent class at UC Berkeley was "The Politics of Education in the 1990s."

Gloria received her associate's degree from Elgin Community College, her bachelor's and master's degrees from Northern Illinois University, and her Ph.D. in Public Policy Analysis from the University of Illinois, Chicago. Her doctoral dissertation, studying the work of public school superintendents, was the impetus for this book.

GWEN E. GROSS

Gwen Gross is superintendent of schools in the Beverly Hills Unified School District in Los Angeles County.

Gwen has served and worked in three states as a teacher, site administrator, college and university professor, and superintendent. In California, following her superintendency of the Hermosa Beach City School District, she moved to Ojai Unified School District in Ventura County, an Annenberg Rural Challenge District, before assuming her position in Beverly Hills in August of 2000.

Gwen has been a principal of a National Blue Ribbon School and has been awarded with the distinction as one of the *Executive Educator's* "Top 100," as one of the "Top One-Hundred Administrators in North America." She has been honored as a Tri-County Superintendent of the Year by the Association of California School Administrators and has served as the chair of the organization's New Superintendents' Symposium.

Gwen has served for several years as a member of the Graduate School of Education and Psychology faculty of Pepperdine University in their Educational Leadership Academy which trains future administrators. She consults with a range of public and private organizations, facilitates workshops, and is a sought-after motivational speaker.

Gwen received her B.A. in Public Address and Communication from the University of Wisconsin, her M.A. in Special Education from the University of Akron, and her Ph.D. in Educational Administration from Kent State University.

RENE S. TOWNSEND

Rene Townsend is a partner in Leadership Associates, a superintendent search firm, an associate in the consulting firm Innovative Strategies, and an instructor and coordinator in the Educational Leadership program at California State University, San Marcos. Rene earned her doctorate in Leadership from Northern Arizona University, master's degree from San Diego State University, and bachelor's from the University of Washington.

Just prior to her current roles, Rene was superintendent of the Coronado and Vista Unified School Districts, both in San Diego County, California. Leading to the superintendency, Rene was an associate superintendent, principal, assistant principal, and teacher at the secondary level.

Rene has served in leadership capacities throughout her career, including terms as Chair of the Association of California School Administrators (ACSA) Superintendents' Committee and as chair of the San Diego and Imperial Counties Superintendents' Committee. She serves on the California Public Schools State Accountability Task Force.

Among the awards Rene has received are the Robert F. Alioto California Instructional Leadership Award, Assembly District Woman of the Year, and San Diego Mediation Center Peacemaker. In professional development, Rene is a consultant to individual school districts, a writer and trainer for the National Leadership Training Associates, and a trainer-presenter for ACSA, the California School Leadership Academy, and other organizations.

Standing out among her career is the period when she led a district during extremely turbulent times following the election of an ultra-conservative board majority. The election immediately thrust the district into national prominence. The most important part, however, for Rene, was that the leadership team and staff never lost their focus on student learning.

PEGGY LYNCH

Dr. Peggy Lynch served seven years as the superintendent for Brea Olinda Unified School District in Orange County, California, and moved to San Dieguito to Union High School District in 2001. She received her doctorate from the University of La Verne in 1993. Prior to her superintendency, Peggy worked in Tustin Unified School District for 24 years. In Tustin, she was a teacher, activities director, assistant principal, high school principal, and assistant superintendent.

Peggy has had numerous leadership roles in the county and in statewide organizations. She was the chair of the Association of California School Administrators (ACSA) Orange County Superintendents for 1999–2000 and has chaired the Superintendents' Symposium Planning Committee, following three years on that committee as well as chairing the New Superintendents' Workshop at the Symposium. In Orange County, Peggy has served on the California School Leadership Academy (CSLA) Advisory Board and the County Superintendent's Advisory Board. She is also a member of the Southern California Superintendents' Group.

Dr. Lynch has been a long-time member of Southern California Women in Education Management (SCWEM) and was selected as the group's Woman of the Year in 1992. She is also a recipient of the Golden Touch Award in 1984 from the Assessment and Treatment Services Center, an award selected by students.

PATRICIA B. NOVOTNEY

Patricia B. Novotney received her doctorate from Pepperdine University (Los Angeles) in Institutional Management. Prior to that she received her master's degree from Chapman College in Orange, California, and her bachelor's degree from Bloomsburg State College in Bloomsburg, Pennsylvania.

Prior to her recent retirement, she spent thirty six years working in the field of education. Her responsibilities included teaching in the Bridgewater-Raritan School District (Somerville, New Jersey) and Fountain Valley School District (Fountain Valley, California), serving as principal in three school districts (Fountain Valley, Ocean View, and Irvine Unified, all in California), and serving as superintendent of Temecula Union School District and superintendent of Temecula Valley Unified School District, California. During her thirteen years as superintendent in Temecula, the district was one of the fastest-growing districts in the state of California. During one four-year period, the district averaged a 34% growth. As an example, in this thirteen-year period the district grew from 1,250 students to 16,000; 2 schools to 16; and 90 total employees to 1,400.

Throughout her professional career, Dr. Novotney received numerous honors, including Kiwanis Club Citizen of the Year, Soroptimist International "Woman of Distinction" Award, Optimist Woman of the Year Award, California State PTA Golden Oak Service Award, Distinguished Alumni Service Award, Bloomsburg State University, One of the Top 10 Most Influential Citizens of Southwest Riverside County, as reported in *The Californian* newspaper, and three-time nominee for Woman of the Year, 37th Senatorial District. Currently she is an educational consultant and an associate professor at the University of LaVerne.

BENITA ROBERTS

Benita B. Roberts, a native of San Bernardino, California, retired after eight years as superintendent of the Jurupa Unified School District, an unincorporated area in western Riverside County. The district enrolls 20,000 students in grades K–12. Her path to the superintendency hardly strayed from the Jurupa Unified School District. She began her career as a classroom teacher there in 1968. She spent a short time as a teacher specialist in mathematics and social studies for the Riverside County Office of Education. She then moved to the Jurupa Unified School District office in 1974, served as instructional coordinator, wrote major proposals for state and federally funded projects, became director of instruction, assistant superintendent of educational services, and has been the superintendent since July 1, 1993.

Ms. Roberts received her B.A. at the University of California, Riverside and her M.A. at California State University, San Bernardino, and pursued her doctorate in educational management at the University of LaVerne. In her first year as superintendent, she led a community and staff committee in developing a strategic plan for the district. More recently, she initiated efforts to develop a Five-Year Facilities Master Plan to accommodate anticipated growth in the community. Ms. Roberts believes that school-reform initiative efforts, whether mandated or by choice, should be viewed positively by the participants impacted by the reform and should result in actual benefits to the sytem. She is proud of the Jurupa Unified School District's effort to implement such reform programs as school choice, school uniforms, class size reduction, standards, and accountability.

Community honors include the 1995 Jurupa Council PTA Honorary Service Award, the 1995 Women of Achievement Proclamation from the Riverside County Board of Supervisors, and the 1997 Jurupa Chamber of Commerce Member of the Year Award. In 1997, she was one of the five Riverside County women honored by the Riverside YWCA as a "Woman of Achievement." In 1999, she was honored by the Rialto Freedom and Culture Society for community service.

LORRAINE GARCY

Dr. Lorraine Garcy has been a superintendent for eleven years. She was superintendent of Rescue Union School District near Sacramento, California, for nine years, and is currently the superintendent of the Livermore Valley Joint Unified School District, which is located in the San Francisco Bay Area. The district has been growing rapidly over the last few years and currently serves 14,000 students in twenty-two schools.

Dr. Garcy received her bachelor of science degree from the State University of New York, Oswego, in education, psychology, and art. She began her teaching career in Fountain Valley, California, and then moved to Goleta, California, where she taught K–4 and GATE. She took a two-year leave of absence to work as an art/psychology/English as a Second Language high school teacher and as the assistant director of the Shiraz Community School in Iran. Upon her return, she taught for three years and then served as a site administrator for four years in the Goleta Union School District. She also completed her master of arts degree from the University of California, Santa Barbara, in administration during this time. In 1985 she moved to Hollister, California, to become assistant superintendent of curriculum and personnel for the Hollister School District. She held this position until she moved to the Rescue Union School District in 1990. In 1993, Dr. Garcy completed her Ed.D. from the University of Southern California with a major in school business.

LIBIA GIL

Dr. Gil has been superintendent of the Chula Vista Elementary School District since 1993. During her tenure, the district has experienced continuous growth, currently serving 23,600 students in thirty-nine schools. She has established five charter schools and fostered the successful implementation of numerous school-change models, such as Accelerated Schools and standards-based instruction. In doing so, she has forged partnerships with Edison Schools Inc., Comer School Development Program, and the Ball Foundation.

Dr. Gil began her teaching career in the Los Angeles Unified School District and has taught in various programs, including English as a Second Language and Gifted and Talented programs. During her teaching experiences, she and two colleagues created a successful K–12 alternative school and numerous alternative classroom programs. She has held a variety of administrative positions, including elementary school principal in the ABC School District and area administrator and assistant superintendent for curriculum and instructional for the Seattle Public Schools. Dr. Gil has a Ph.D. in Curriculum and Instruction from the University of Washington.

Dr. Gil has been recognized as the outstanding educator of the year by the Chula Vista Chamber. Currently, she is a mentor superintendent and board member for the Harvard Superintendents Program. She is also serving on the advisory board for the Wallace Foundation's "Leaders Count" program.